Raising Good Children

Raising Good Children

Anne Jesper

Ⓛ

The Lutterworth Press

Published by
The Lutterworth Press
P.O. Box 60
Cambridge
CB1 2NT
England

e-mail: **publishing@lutterworth.com**
website: **http://www.lutterworth.com**

ISBN 0 7188 3037 7 paperback

British Library Cataloguing in Publication Data:
A catalogue record is available from the British Library.

First published by the Lutterworth Press 2004

Printed in the United Kingdom
by Athenaeum Press

To my children, grandchildren
and all the children that I have taught
who have unwittingly provided material for this book;
to the friends who have helped with advice,
comments and anecdotes,
and to my husband for his endless patience
whilst I was occupied with writing

CONTENTS

Introduction

It is now over thirty years since I first had the desire to write this book and the initial research for it was done in the late 1960s, but the idea was shelved in 1971 when we started a business, which, together with bringing up a family, took all my time. Now it is being written from the perspective of a grandmother as well as that of a mother, but sadly, the need for such a book is even more pressing now than it was thirty years ago.

Many of us share a deep concern over various aspects of children's upbringing and of the pernicious social influences which impinge upon our children, teenagers and young adults. We cringe at toddlers who scream until they get their own way; we are appalled at the lack of respect shown to adults by disgruntled and bored school children; we despair over youngsters who drift into drug taking, violence and other crime and we weep for teenage mums.

Why have we failed to come to grips with these issues? Why have we failed to develop more helpful and constructive attitudes in so many young people? Why have we not understood the factors that will instil proper self-control?

We give attention to developing crops that will yield better harvests, yet not enough thought to cultivating the good qualities in children that will enable them to develop into caring individuals who will give a better yield in the citizenship field. We are concerned about environmental pollution, yet little is done to clear up mental pollution. We tackle crime by building more prisons and giving stiffer sentences when we should be preventing the development of criminal tendencies in young minds. We do research into genes, yet none into kindness, we develop clones in the plant and animal kingdoms yet are dismayed when the violent models portrayed on TV and on computer screens produce their clones in real life. We immunise children to protect them from disease, but neglect the thought habits that would help to develop an immunity to temptation. We hear so much about the need to save our physical environment, but not nearly enough about the need to restore a wholesome mental environment.

The factors that have led up to current shifting societal values had their origins in the desire to start afresh after World War II. Traditional values, beliefs and morals were progressively discarded in favour of experimenting with new life styles. Sufficient time has now elapsed for us to take a realistic view of where this approach has left us and at the results which have ripped apart our society. The reality is a far cry from the joy that sexual freedom was supposed to confer and the fulfilment that was predicted from self-expression. The reality is a loss of self-worth, heartaches, shattered lives and single parent families. The areas of deprivation touch the moral, intellectual, social and physical aspects of children's lives.

In the 1970s the word "mores" made its appearance as a substitute for morals. Mores are defined as "the customs, habits or moral assumptions of a community" and imply that people should make their own moral judgements. Moral law was no longer recognised and young people who lacked both the necessary knowledge and experience, were encouraged to make their own moral assumptions while adults abdicated their responsibility to pass on the wisdom of the past.

The time has surely come when we should acknowledge that future generations deserve something better. They deserve that the hole in the moral ozone be repaired by examining and correcting the mental factors that lie at the root of today's troubled society. They deserve that parents, guardians, teachers and mentors learn to recognise and to utilise the unseen spiritual force for good which at present is largely unrecognised and unacknowledged. I have found the nature of this power to be most clearly enunciated in the writings of Mary Baker Eddy whose inspired and scientific approach to Christianity illumines the practical value of the Bible. The Bible and Mrs. Eddy's writings helped me immeasurably in the upbringing of my own family.

My aims are to awaken in my readers a greater awareness of life's potential for good and of how much can be achieved by spiritualising one's thoughts and also to share some insights into the value of the Bible as a resource for spiritual and moral guidance. Tolstoy once said of the Bible, "I cannot think how the education of children would be possible if the Book of books did not exist."

In the 16th century, there was a determined attempt to deprive the British people of the Bible when William Tyndale was persecuted by both King and clergy and finally martyred for translating the Bible into English. A second attempt came in the twentieth century with scientific systems which have no place for the things of the Spirit in their physically based world. It is up to us, the present parents and grandparents, to ensure that future generations are not deprived of the very book that has been the backbone of our culture, our society, and of the morality in which our spirituality has its roots. When the Bible is quoted in this book, the quotations are from the King James (Authorised) Version, unless otherwise stated. GNB refers to the Good News Bible, NEB to the New English Bible and NIV to the New International Version.

Repairing the damage that has been done may take time, but solutions are there and in the long term, our hope for a better future for our children lies in starting with the very young, to give them better standards and ideals and the security that comes from understanding something of the nature of God and that they are loved by Him/Her.

Despite the challenges, the present time is a wonderful era in which to be bringing up children, for never before have so many opportunities been open to a rising generation. Air travel and the Internet are opening up the world in ways that were unimagined to previous generations; children's books have never been so imaginative and abundant as they are now; opportunities are there for women to make their contribution in the world, the ideal of world peace is being more widely sought and barriers to prosperity are being removed. We now need to demolish the barriers to moral and spiritual progress for the sake of children everywhere.

> Train up a child in the way he should go: and when he is old, he will not depart from it.   Proverbs 22:6

I. The Power Within

God is always at work in you.   Philippians 2:13, GNB

In the year 1885 Edward Joseph Flanagan, was born into an Irish farming family. One day the young Eddie was helping his father to herd the cows who suddenly stampeded towards a swamp. "Bad cows" yelled the boy, but his father corrected him. "There's no such thing as a bad cow," he said, "they just don't know any better."

When Eddie grew up, he was ordained as a Roman Catholic priest and emigrated to America and found fame as the founder of Boy's Town, near Omaha, Nebraska, where homeless boys were housed and educated. Father Flanagan, as he was then known, transformed the lives of thousands of boys who, like the cows, didn't know any better. His biographers, Fulton and Will Oursler, wrote, "His ability to transform the toughest of juvenile delinquents, so-called, into co-operative and socially adjusted young men of contented integrity, shines like a beam of light in a darkened scene." His methods were simple, so simple that they puzzled many experts, but they were grounded in his firm belief that there's no such thing as a bad boy.

When he was faced with the outward appearance of defiance, insolence and obstinacy, Father Flanagan knew that these characteristics were only apparent because the boys hadn't been taught any better, so he treated them with the love and respect that their God-given identity, hidden though it was, warranted. This approach aroused within his boys feelings of co-operation and responsibility which had previously been dormant and brought to light the fact that a power for good was present within the consciousness of his boys.

The presence of a higher power is the
neglected resource in raising good children.

This higher power is wholly good; it is ever-present and is spiritual in nature. It can be likened to radio waves in that it is invisible to the physical senses, has always been there, but until discovered and utilised, is of no benefit to man. Successful educators feel instinctively how to use that inner power which makes children good and obedient, but it is a sad fact that at the beginning of the twenty first century this power of God is not acknowledged as an invaluable aid in the upbringing of children, and that the example of someone like Father Flanagan is not better known, nor his methods taught in teacher training courses. Orthodox theories of education leave God out, which is why Father Flanagan always distrusted them. His successes point not to a power that might or might not intervene in human affairs by means of a miracle, but to a God who is ever present Love, waiting for men to utilise the goodness He pours into every human heart.

What came so naturally to Father Flanagan, with his outstanding compassion and spiritual perception does not always come so easily to the rest of us. At the end of a school year, a certain teacher was dismayed to find that a pupil, who had been a troublemaker all the way up the school where she taught, was to be in her class for the forthcoming year. She instinctively felt that this girl's behaviour could not be indicative of her true nature but found that to have real confidence in what she intuitively felt to be true, demanded a lot of prayer, in fact she prayed throughout the summer holidays. On the day before school was to reopen, the teacher went to prepare her classroom and was surprised to see the girl she had been praying about, come up to the window and peep in. "Hello ——-" she said, "I'm looking forward to having you in my class this year." By this time, she really was regarding the girl in a different light and genuinely meant what she said. The girl looked quite startled, said no more and went away.

On the following day, after morning school, the girl lingered behind after the other children had gone. "Did you really mean what you said yesterday, about being pleased to have me in your class?" she asked. The teacher assured her that she did mean it and from that moment on, the girl was a changed character and caused no more trouble.

A teacher friend of mine had a similar experience when a boy who had been regarded as the terror of the school arrived in her class. My friend took a stand to see beyond the outward appearance. It took great mental discipline to do this but she persisted. During the year the boy was in her class there was such marked improvement in his behaviour that the boy's mother came to the school to express her thanks. She said that when she had asked the boy what caused the change, he replied that Ms — didn't expect him to be a naughty boy.

Like Father Flanagan, both these teachers had a deep love for the children in their care and could not accept that they were intrinsically bad. Like him, they saw something deeper than the outward appearances and what they saw was more real to them than the evidence before their eyes and the children responded accordingly.

Seeing something good that is unseen to the physical senses is seeing with the heart, not with the eyes; it is regarding others with love. It is spiritual perception of that inner power and it can be described like this: Imagine someone had a blue car and this car was wrapped in yellow cellophane. When you looked at the car, you'd see a green car. This wouldn't mean that the original colour of the car had changed, merely that its outward appearance had. Someone who was unaware of the cellophane might think at first that the car was green, but anyone who knew it was wrapped, would realise immediately that it was still blue. In like manner, anyone who is convinced of the innate goodness of children has no need to accept the outward appearance of disruptive, disobedient or rude boys and girls. St. Paul put it this way when he wrote to the inhabitants of Corinth, "…we look not at the things which are seen, but at the things which are not seen: for the things which are seen are temporal; but the things which are not seen are eternal." God does control His children, but you have to know how to get rid of that outer layer if you are to be able to witness that control. The power of divine Love, operating through a compassionate adult has the power to melt away that outer layer and reveal the true colour (character) underneath.

The experience of a friend of mine who was a problem child as he progressed through junior school is a case in point. He told me that he remembers crouching behind the settee, hiding from the policemen who came round about the fire he had started, while his mother assured them that she would see that there was no more arson, a promise that in her heart, she knew would be hard to keep. The time then came for him to move to secondary school, which was warned in advance about his disruptive behaviour. (He told me that he was disruptive because he was bright and was not challenged by his lessons.) The head of the secondary school decided to put him under the wing of one particular teacher. This teacher took a genuine interest in the boy, didn't treat him as though he was a bad boy and even did all sorts of interesting things with him after school. That teacher turned his life around and a lad who might have ended up in jail, has now forged out for himself a most interesting career with a high degree of personal responsibility. He says that he will always be grateful to that teacher who believed in him when others didn't – the teacher who looked through the yellow cellophane and saw the blue car.

Another simple example of how to arouse the power that works in us occurred in a junior school. A teacher's aide was helping in a class that was being disrupted by an unruly child, so she beckoned the child to her and whispered into her ear, "I know a secret about you, do you know what it is?" The girl didn't, so she went on, "I know what a good girl you are. You know you're a good girl, don't you?" The girl nodded. "Now you are to *be* very good, then maybe the teacher will discover the secret too. Will you do that?" The girl said she would and was no problem for the rest of the session. Children need to be helped to have good feelings about themselves. Can you imagine being in a crowd of people who disliked you and believed you to be bad? Can you imagine how differently you would behave when you were with people who admired and loved you?

This mental approach can work equally effectively with groups as with individuals. A speaker was invited to give a talk to some senior pupils in a school. On his arrival the teacher in charge said, "It's very nice of you to come, but you won't get anywhere with this lot, they are really hopeless; you'll never get any questions, they are so unintelligent." The speaker, however, was well practised in the art of seeing through that yellow outer layer and his talk was followed by some good, thoughtful questions. Afterwards the teacher asked, "How on earth did you do that? I've never seen this lot like that before!" The speaker's reply was, "To be frank, I did not see them as you do, and they responded naturally."

In all the foregoing instances, what occurred was that the "power within" was reactivated.

When the Office for Standards in Education (OFSTED) reported on a school in my area that was below standard, the inspectors stated that nearly 20% of the lessons in this school were unsatisfactory because they were badly planned and because teachers *had low expectations of pupils' work and behaviour*. (My emphasis). The teachers in this school had been fooled by the yellow cellophane.

Sadly, either through exasperation or despair and through ignorance of the inner power, the older generation frequently leave something to be desired when coping with troublesome behaviour on the part of youths. In resolving difficult situations, it is vital to avoid a "you against them" scenario. Instead, everyone needs to feel that it is "you and them" working together on the problem.

One spring morning I saw a little girl, hardly old enough to be out on her own, picking crocuses in the centre of the village where I live and it so happened that I had planted the crocuses. I could have run out, shouting at her to stop and no doubt she would have done so. She would have been upset, run away and I wouldn't have done anything to help her to see why what she was doing was wrong.

Instead, I went quietly up to her and crouched down to her level (its always a bit intimidating if someone is towering over you). I spoke to her about how pretty the crocuses looked, growing in the grass and how I had worked hard in the autumn planting the corms. I said that if she had done all that work so that everyone could enjoy the flowers, she wouldn't want someone coming along and just taking them all away, would she? She looked very repentant and just said, "No". I felt that she would never do such a thing again and we parted on a happy note.

On another occasion, when I was returning from a visit to London, I boarded a train at St. Pancras station and sat down. Everyone in the carriage was sitting quietly reading or snoozing when a youth in leathers came in and shoved his belongings on the overhead rack, then down came his radio on to the table and up went his boots on to the opposite seat. He turned up the radio and settled comfortably. Everyone began to bristle and you could just feel the antagonism. I paused for a moment's prayer to feel assured that inner goodness was present – that there must be a responsive chord, then I went over to the young man. I sat down beside him, smiled and made a remark about liking music. He smiled back so I added that probably a lot of us on the train enjoyed music, but as tastes differed, did he think he could turn the volume down a little? He agreed that he could, and I suggested that if he bought earphones it might help for a future occasion. "Oh, I've got some," he said and reached up to the rack to get them down. Having got that part settled, I then mentioned that I too like putting my feet up on train seats, but I did take my shoes off first. His feet came down in a flash, I went back to my seat and the pleasant atmosphere returned.

It is an inescapable fact that prevailing adult attitudes and in particular the attitudes of parents and teachers, shape the attitudes and behaviour of children, either to free all concerned to feel

the power of goodness, or to let it remain shrouded in disobedience. On the one hand, this may be a challenging fact to face, but on the other hand, it is encouraging to know that improving one's own attitude will inevitably find a responsive chord in a child. Never give up on a child, a breakthrough in behaviour may take time, but go on loving the goodness of the child's inner self and you will win.

Today, as in ancient Athens, when St. Paul saw an altar "To the unknown God" the nature of the one God, the source of inner goodness in mankind, still remains largely unknown, which is why His influence in human affairs is not more widely acknowledged.

In the world today, seemingly so dominated by the secular, can any of us find a logical explanation for ever present, innate goodness in men — and in children? I believe we can. Instead of training telescopes to outer space to learn the origin of our being, we would do better to focus our mental microscopes on the inner space of our consciousness. Such physically intangible things as conscience, inspiration and intuition give us a practical basis from which to start.

The conscience that pricks us when we err is felt by most people. Conscience must have an origin, so what is more natural than to accept it as the voice of God? Some people develop their conscience to the extent that they cannot perform antisocial acts; others subdue their conscience until its voice is no longer audible to them. A vital part of raising good children is to make them aware of their conscience and to guide them to obey it, for conscience grows stronger with use.

Then there is inspiration, often needed by parents to help them cope in difficult moments. When we are inspired, we always feel that inspiration is something that *comes* to us. Listen carefully when you next hear an author, artist or inventor being interviewed. If they are asked where they get their ideas from, they never say, "Oh my brain worked really hard to produce that." They invariably reply, "The ideas just came to me." People naturally describe their creative thought processes in this way but God is not usually associated with it, yet if thoughts come to us, they come from somewhere. Anxiety, doubt and pride are the enemies that prevent us from feeling inspired. They need replacing by trust, humility and a willingness to listen to that ever-present inner voice.

The intuitive sense that tells us to take a certain course of action – the "gut" feelings we all have is another significant mental phenomenon. When developed, intuition is invaluable in raising children. It is becoming increasingly fashionable for experts to encourage new mothers, for instance, to rely on their intuition in caring for their babies rather than to turn to human advice. People who trust their intuition find that, like conscience, it becomes stronger with use and a reliable guide to the proper course of action.

It is quite fascinating to look for real-life stories that illustrate the value of intuition. One of my favourites is the story of Gladys Aylward, which was filmed under the title *The Inn of the Sixth Happiness*. The book *The Small Woman* on which the film was based, tells that in the early 1900s, Gladys left her post as a parlour maid in London – much against the wishes of the mission that she wanted to represent – to go to China as a missionary. Her stay in China coincided with the Sino-Japanese war and at one time Gladys was forced to flee from the advancing Japanese soldiers. She had with her a nine-year old orphan boy and a teenage girl, and they were aiming to escape from the town of Chin Shui by the East Gate. We read, "They had walked no further than 300 yards when Gladys felt the stirrings of a strange uneasiness in her mind. She began to worry. They had two miles to cover before they could reach the rocky shelter of the mountains, and some instinctive sense, some mental telepathy winked a series of warning signals along the corridor of her brain. There was no visual reason for the oppression of fear she suddenly experienced, but she believed implicitly in her intuitions. . . . 'We're going back,' she announced loudly." They changed direction to leave by the West Gate; shortly afterwards shots were heard as Japanese soldiers arrived at the East Gate.

Incidents like that can help parents when faced with little boys climbing rocks or up trees. "Don't go any higher than you feel is safe," I have often said, then I trust that the child will hear that intuitive sense guiding him. This is a wonderful way to keep children safe, but I would also stress to children that they must never go high to show off. Showing off is a form of pride which will block that intuitive sense and would endanger them.

Watch the daily papers when accidents are reported and you will discover examples of situations when victims of a disaster or someone close to them, had a sense of impending danger or had an inner prompting that, if acted upon, would have kept them, or others, safe.

After the Dunblane massacre in Scotland when thirteen schoolchildren and a teacher were shot dead, the policeman who had re-issued Thomas Hamilton, the gunman, with his gun licence said that he had felt instinctively that here was a man who shouldn't have guns, but that you need more than a hunch to be able to refuse a license.

Before the launch of the ill-fated Challenger flight, some NASA officials were reported to have felt a distinct sense of unease about the launch. In both these instances, if those concerned had known that these intuitions were communications from God, and acted upon them, tragic losses of life could have been averted. When the Arabs who flew their planes into the World Trade Centre received their pilot's training in Florida, the instructors were aware that there was something "fishy" about them. We shall never know what might have been changed if this feeling had been followed by an investigation into the background of those men.

It may be unfashionable to link such things as conscience, intuition and inspiration with a divine source, yet not one of these has ever been located beneath a skull bone; not one of them has ever been dissected by a surgeon's knife, and it seems a reasonable proposition to say that they originate not in a human, but in a divine Mind. Some scientists and a number of religious thinkers have put forward the concept that God is Mind and if you look for instances in nature of a supreme intelligence or Mind, you find it. Consider migrating birds, for example. How do they remember the route they should take? I don't believe they do. I believe they are responding instinctively to a supreme intelligence and that maybe they could teach humans a thing or two about trust. The orderliness of the planets can be regarded as more evidence of the presence of a spiritual intelligence, of a Mind that is God.

Consider for a moment this simple drawing:

What is it?
It could be a ball,
just a circle,
the moon,
or even an orange.

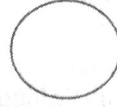

Now add something to that drawing
like this:

When the drawing is complete,
everyone can recognise
that it is the sun.

God can be likened to the sun, which is central to our being, and good impulses can be likened to the rays of light, which emanate from the sun. The second picture illustrates this relationship between the divine Mind and us. Because of the evil that men do in this world, many people doubt that there is a God – the round circle then has nothing to identify it. When men are good, it becomes easier to believe in God, therefore we need to express our godlike natures in order for God's presence to be more clearly felt.

The moral sense, including conscience, results from mental receptivity to the voice of God, therefore morality and spirituality are inseparable; ethical human behaviour is our link to the divine Mind and acting ethically facilitates an awareness of the power of goodness within. When the physically intangible conscience, intuition or inspiration appear to be hidden in some individuals, that should not deceive us into believing they are absent.

Children should be taught about the unseen presence of God and to acknowledge Him as the origin of their good thoughts. They should be taught that they are God's children and that God's children must be good, like God is. This is the spiritual fact about us all and it is a sacred duty to make this spiritual fact evident in our own lives and in the lives of our children. Adults as well as children need learn how to listen to God and to obey good impulses.

You may feel at this point that there are obvious problems with this line of reasoning. There are certainly two problems that deserve our consideration but to go into them in depth is beyond the scope of this book.

PROBLEM 1

We are taught that thoughts originate in the brain.

At one time, people believed that their thinking resided in the stomach. At a later period the heart was accepted as the origin of consciousness, hence the phrase, "to learn by heart."

As human knowledge increases, theories that are accepted at one time are adapted or even dropped in the light of fresh developments, therefore might it not be possible that in the future a different theory may be adopted regarding the origin of our thoughts? Presumably when people still believed that their thought processes were in the stomach or the heart, they would have strenuously resisted any suggestion that the head was the seat of intelligence, for that which is accepted by the majority is regarded as fact until hard evidence to the contrary is found, and even then, changing entrenched beliefs is not easy as Copernicus and Galileo discovered when trying to convince people that the sun revolved around the earth and not vice versa. Therefore it is not surprising to find some resistance to the idea that God supplies our thoughts, yet once you become "tuned in" to His wavelength, the plainer the signals become and the more convinced you are of being the recipient of ideas, rather than the creator of them. You tune in to the divine Mind by desiring to be good, by putting aside personal opinions, by cultivating a receptive state of mind and by being willing to act upon what you hear.

Wilder Penfield, an American neurosurgeon who has conducted extensive research on the brain stated, "I, like other scientists, have struggled to prove that brain accounts for the mind." Other researchers have commented that the relationship between consciousness and brain is still an enigma and have queried whether consciousness is something beyond a bio-chemical reaction in the brain. The observations of those who have had Near Death Experiences (NDEs) lend weight to the idea that consciousness is something beyond grey matter. The majority of these experiences have occurred in hospital and patients have been able to give accurate accounts of what happened in the room and of procedures carried out on their bodies whilst they were clinically brain dead. Dr Sam Parnia, one of two doctors who set up the first ever study of NDEs in the UK, referred to these experiences at a doctors' conference held in London in September 2002. He said, "These patients should not be capable of thought if thoughts come from the brain, because they have no brain function. In fact there has never been any proof that the brain generates thought." Such observations are of great significance because they herald a profound change in human belief about the origin of thoughts.

PROBLEM 2

If God is sending us good thoughts,
what about the bad thoughts?

I like to think of it in this way: If you, personally, really wanted to be kind to everyone for just one hour, you could do that, couldn't you? You could exert the mental strength to shut the door of your thinking to any unkindness and be nice for an hour, and if you could do it, others could too. Now just imagine that everyone in the whole world resolved to be kind for one hour, then during that hour there would be no unkindness throughout the whole world. Where would the unkindness have gone? It would have been overcome by the kindness we had resolved to show. It is within our power to prove that evil thoughts do not have the force behind them that good thoughts have because we are capable of eradicating them.

We hear it said that we all have a dark side, and it cannot be disputed that everyone either accepts the presence of evil in their consciousness or they strive to do something about it. Those who do strive to do something about it and make a systematic effort to control their thinking and to strengthen the good in their thoughts, discover that, in time, evil thoughts have less hold on them and their minds are more filled with goodness. An individual who makes a sustained effort to overcome a bad temper, for example, will in time find themselves less prone to violent outbursts. This is a fact that can only be discovered, if the necessary conditions are fulfilled. Side by side with developing an awareness of the power of good in their thoughts, children also need instruction in how to stand up to wrong thoughts. This theme is expanded in chapter 3 in the section "Shutting the Door."

Taking responsibility for one's own thoughts is seldom considered, let alone taught to children, but the concept of being in control of one's thoughts is most attractive to young people, for it gives a feeling of empowerment. To nurture a child's ability to think for themselves is one of the most valuable tools parents can develop in their children. Children can then discover how to remain calm in times of confusion and how to maintain love in their hearts when facing intimidation. The child who learns how to think with good and pure thoughts in his early years is developing his relationship with the divine Mind, and consequently is assembling useful ammunition for coping with bullying and for countering the so-called lure of drugs in later years.

Fear is the main enemy that prevents proper thought control, for it has the apparent effect of paralysing constructive ideas. When a schoolteacher feels a class slipping out of control, fear says it may be worse next time. When a toddler makes a rumpus in public, fear may whisper to the parent, "You can't do anything with him," and the intuition that would solve the problem is not heard. Turning to the divine Mind and trusting the innate goodness of man helps to stop fear in its tracks.

People are not born bad. If it were true that problem children (and problem adults) were physically programmed by their genes to be as they are, they would be lost souls with little or no hope of ever being able to improve their lot and I don't think that deep down anyone really believes this to be the case; we instinctively feel that there should always be hope of regeneration and reformation. As soon as the medical faculty has pronounced a disease to be incurable, they set about developing a cure. In our hearts, most of us do not believe in the finality of incurability; we feel that healing and reform must always be a possibility.

When one thinks of the size of a human egg at the moment of conception – roughly the size of a pin-head, it can stretch incredulity somewhat to accept that all human characteristics from the colour of the eyes to mathematical ability is encapsulated in that tiny little spot of protoplasm. Have you ever noted that adopted children frequently grow to be as like their parents as other children and that even long married husband and wives sometimes look like brother and sister? I therefore find it logical to believe that children take after their parents, not because of a law of heredity, but because the parents' views shape their children's minds. In time, what's going on in your mind will inevitably be revealed on your face.

If we are to train future generations into better ways, we need to understand more not of physical, but of mental anatomy. We need to acknowledge and harness the spiritual power of God operating in consciousness, and which is recognised in qualities such as purity, kindness and unselfishness. If anti-social elements are to be eradicated from our society, they must first be eradicated in mortal thoughts and good thought habits established which will be manifested in purposeful, constructive and compassionate lives.

When lives are turned around, as Father Flanagan turned around so many young lives, the basic change is always in the thinking of the person concerned. It is always attitudes that need to change for lives to be improved. How we think is at the root of everything that happens in the world. How children think determines whether their behaviour is either good or bad, therefore in order to raise good children, it is necessary to teach children how to think in ways that will result in good behaviour. Children need not only to be taught the difference between right and wrong, but must also be educated to love the right. To know the difference between right and wrong is not much use without gaining a desire to do what is right.

It is when the inner goodness present in children is not nurtured that the poisonous weeds of selfishness, greed, disobedience and the like flourish unchecked, and the harvest is not a pleasant one, whereas proper cultivation of the inner self transforms character.

In order to return to a more stable society the moral rot that set in several decades ago must be stopped by changing the adult attitudes that have allowed undesirable elements in society to flourish. Double standards must be rejected and more faith placed in intuition, conscience, inspiration and common sense.

The greatest need is for a better understanding of God as the divine Mind and of man's mental link with his Creator.

We should not therefore surrender our ideals to the prevailing customs, but should endeavour to close the gap between those ideals and our actions. If future generations are to have higher ethical standards, a number of things will have to change:

· The inherent goodness of children must be acknowledged and nurtured.

· The spiritual power that will make this goodness apparent must be utilised.

· Marriage must again be cherished as the institution that provides the best environment for children and the ideal of chastity before marriage, and fidelity within it needs to be restored.

· Less attention should be focussed on the body and more on controlling thought.

· Children must not only learn the difference between right and wrong, they must also be taught to love doing right.

· Adults must provide better role models for children if the scourge of drug taking is to be eliminated.

· The public must demand that the media as a whole and especially the entertainment industry must show greater social responsibility and clean up its act.

· The neglected gems in the Bible must be re-polished.

The following chapters share some ideas on how these goals may be achieved.

Here is a force which history proves to have been the greatest power in the development of men. We have never seriously studied it as we have the material forces. In the future, scientists will turn their laboratories over to the study of God and prayer and the spiritual forces which as yet have scarcely been touched.

Dr. Charles Steinmetz

II. Functional Families

Our birth is but a sleep and a forgetting;
The Soul that rises with us, our life's Star
Hath elsewhere had its setting,
And cometh from afar:
Not in entire forgetfulness,
And not in utter nakedness,
But trailing clouds of glory do we come
From God, who is our home.
                    William Wordsworth, 'Intimations of Immortality'

When a new babe is born, the parents are not being presented with a blank slate on which they may write, they are getting a precious God-created individual who already possesses all the good qualities he needs. It is the parents' privilege to provide an environment where these good qualities can blossom; they must preserve the innate innocence, purity and goodness which every little child brings into this world, be they given or chosen (adopted). Human birth may sever the child's physical union with his mother, but it has not the slightest effect on his mental union with God, his divine Father-Mother, the source of his good thoughts and ideas, his conscience, intuition and inspiration. This union can never be severed.

The knowledge that your child has a direct line to the divine Mind, who constantly supplies him with good thoughts, is an immense help in lifting the weight of responsibility from parents. A mother who wanted her small daughter to understand that she was God's child, as well as hers found it difficult to put into words what she meant to convey. However, the little girl got the message, "Oh I see!" she said, "You're really the baby-sitter." Parenthood should be a joy and the "baby sitters" should aim to produce perfect morals in children – why settle for less? Excellence is not an act but a habit and habits either for good or bad are often established very early in life, so let them be established for good!

These are the inescapable duties of parents and when these duties are not fulfilled schoolteachers have an unfair load on their shoulders. Schools and teachers are there in order that special skills may be learned and knowledge acquired that is generally beyond the scope of the home. Teachers have a supporting role in the teaching of morals but should not have to spend their time and the time of the disciplined children in their care, in keeping unruly children in order.

Morals are caught, as well as taught, therefore parents need to exercise the utmost care that they provide the very best example of which they are capable. Sound morals give a child roots – the security of finding that what *feels* right within coincides with the rules being imposed from without. If young children are being expected to do things that are patently unfair they will, understandably, rebel. If, on the other hand, they feel comfortable with the standards that are expected of them, they are secure. That is not to say that there won't be times when they will test the limits – of course they will, wouldn't you? They do need to know that limits mean limits. The foundations for this are best begun in small ways very soon after birth and by the time a child is walking, he should understand that the word "No" means what it says and that flouting it is not an option.

Consistency, firmness and discipline give a child a framework so he knows where he stands. Having a regular bedtime helps a child to develop a sense of order and saves many an argument. Too much "freedom" does not make a child feel loved and secure. A woman who was brought up in a troubled home told me that as a child she could play outside for as long as she wished; other children were called in by their mothers to have their tea, but no-one called her in. The other kids thought it was great, being able to play out for as long as you wanted, but she didn't, she just wanted someone to tell her what to do. Children need the security of an adult being in charge, giving instructions and seeing that these instructions are carried through.

There is a saying in Africa that "it takes a village to raise a child", and it is unfortunate today that a sense of community is often lacking in the more "advanced" cultures. It does help if neighbours and friends have similar standards to your own. When my children were small, most mothers were not out at work and I used to visit friends with little ones so the children could play together and sometimes we would care for each other's children. We had an understanding amongst ourselves that any mother was free to rebuke any-one else's child if the need arose. We all wanted our children to be helpful and polite and in this way the children had consistent standards whoever was around.

Children need people to look up to, they need good examples. Present role models – often pop stars or sportsmen – all too often have "feet of clay". Footballers and pop idols are not always positive influences on their young fans.

Even the simplest role models of yesterday are being swept away – children's reading books no longer show Mummy washing the dishes and Daddy going out to work – it's no longer politically correct. Although the roles of the sexes in a family undoubtedly benefit by being more flexible than in times past, in most families the basic framework of the traditional roles still works best, for it comes more naturally to most women to oversee domestic matters than it does to most men. It is well-known that some dads who are the primary care-givers have proved that they can be good "mums" and some single mums rise to the challenge of being both father and mother, for there is no barrier to a man being gentle and tender, nor to a woman being strong and courageous, but we should ask ourselves whether children from one-parent families, more than others, aren't being deprived by having the traditional role models removed in this way.

Everyone has a distinct individuality and a unique contribution that they can make in their family, and to their world. In one family I know, the three-year old was told, "We all have a job to do in this family. Daddy's job is to go to work and earn money for us to buy our food and clothes. Mummy's job is to look after the house and to look after you and the baby and your job is to be kind to everyone." In such ways, children learn to value themselves and others.

From the loving example of one family a whole state becomes loving.
Attributed to Confucius

The Mental Atmosphere

If a home is to have the mental atmosphere in which children can be happy – and all children have the right to a happy home – then whenever possible parents should make every effort to sort out any disagreements of their own when the children are in bed. "Not in front of the children" should be the rule.

A happy home atmosphere spills over into the school, into the community and ultimately into the world, it's that important! A first time visitor to a home said to the wife and mother, "You don't shout at your children, do you?" Somewhat surprised, the hostess replied that she didn't. "I thought not," said the visitor, "You can tell by the atmosphere when you come into this house." Maybe the tone of one's voice, more than any other one thing, affects the home atmosphere.

Shouting at the children (or your partner) inevitably worsens what is obviously an already fraught situation. Shouting is counter-productive because it is inflammatory, instead of calming. Worse still, if it becomes a habit, your children will quickly learn either to ignore or to emulate it. How can we expect our children to control their behaviour if we are unable to control ours? The tendency to shout can be overcome by persisting in the desire to remain calm. If you really want to be calm, then you can, because peace is God-given. Nobody lacks inner peace, but they frequently need to activate it and every home needs a peacemaker.

In dealings with both children and adults, I've trained myself to ask inwardly "What will my action (or my words) do to his thinking? Will I make him feel inferior or will I bolster his self-esteem? Will I help him to solve a problem, or will I be rubbing his nose in it?" An ability to foresee the effects of something you say or do guides you when tackling tricky situations. If a certain course of action will make a child feel despairing and hopeless, then it is never the right course to take. If, however, he needs to be made to feel really sorry for what he has done, then words that reduce him to tears may be the ones that have the needed effect. Every time a child is admonished, it should be done in a manner which awakens the desire to be good. An incident that happened once when I was teaching very little ones in Sunday School never fails to make me smile. One pupil developed a liking for going under the table, instead of sitting on his chair. Various means that I tried to get him out had all failed. These small children had been taught that God gives them good thoughts and that these were to be obeyed, so I finally thought to say, "John, what is God telling you to do?" "GET OUT" he replied promptly – and got out.

A simple technique for keeping a pleasant tone in the home, is what my husband calls, "Upshutmanship" – in other words, just shut up about anything that really doesn't need to be said, and which would possibly cause unhappiness, for silence is better than censure. Have you ever heard parents say bad things about their child in front of that child? That is the worse possible thing to do. NEVER let a child hear you speak critically about him to a third person. Admonish in private whenever possible. Always build your children's self-esteem and avoid comparisons with other children, whether they be siblings, friends or even children you meet in the street.

A multitude of problems in human relationships are caused by individuals not valuing themselves, and what they uniquely have to offer to their friends, their families and their communities. Children need both appropriate praise and encouragement. Winston Churchill's mother Jenny once said, "Treat your friends as you do your pictures and place them in their best light." That is something parents should do for their children.

One mother I know praises her little girl for obedience by saying "Good listening Ellie" and when she comes up with a good idea, she says, "Good thinking Ellie".

The arrival of a second baby always calls for great tact, but if this important event is handled with thoughtfulness for the first child's feelings, there is no need for jealousy. In one family I know, the older child, a little boy, was well prepared and spoke often to the unborn baby. "Hello baby," he was taught to say, "I'm your brother." A "toy baby" (not a "doll" because this was a little boy) with a little bath was purchased before the birth, then when Mummy bathed the new baby, brother bathed his toy baby. Parents can watch to see that when friends admire the new baby, they speak first to the older child. Lots of love and praise for the older child will do wonders.

"Order is heaven's first law" says the Bible. I have always equated heaven with harmony and as I wanted harmony to prevail in my home, I always made an effort to be tidy. Tidiness and orderliness help to convey a feeling of calm, which is conducive to good behaviour. I was blessed by having the world's most orderly man as my father and as a child I remember him saying "A place for everything and everything in its place." It seemed natural to me that everything must have its place – it was some considerable time before it dawned on me that a place for everything wasn't something that happened as if by magic. Things only have their place because they have been allocated one, so do be sure to give everything a proper "home".

When my children were small and the house had become a tip, we made it a game each afternoon to get it tidy "before Daddy comes home." As Mary Poppins knew, make the job a game, put in an element of fun, and children will respond. Necessary jobs need not become chores. I was impressed once when visiting the home of a friend and something was lost. The young son in the house brightly said, "I'll tell you the easiest way to find it." I was interested! "You just tidy everything away, then you find it," he said, "My mummy taught me that."

Order in actions is important too. "*First* you eat two more spoonfuls of vegetables, *then* you can have some pudding." "Put your things away, *then* I'll read you a story." "Go to the toilet, *then* you can play."

When bringing up young children, as with other jobs, the first thing is to keep "on top" yourself, for if you are worried, tired or fed up, your children will suffer. With this in mind, as well as for the sake of my children, we had "Quiet Time" in our home for very many years. I was an only child and when I was small, had to learn to be happy with my own company. I found in adulthood what a valuable asset this is and was determined that our family, even though they had siblings, should have the benefit of spending time in their own company. Every child benefits from the opportunity, right from the start, to have time to reflect without distraction – something that is valued by balanced individuals of all ages. So we had Quiet Time for an hour after lunch when each child had to remain in his or her own room and entertain him or herself. The one thing that was forbidden was any sort of contact with each other. Lunch was at 12 noon, we were finished by half past and Quiet Time was until 1.30 when "Watch With Mother" started on TV. 12.30 was my deadline if I was to get a decent quiet time for myself. It worked very well right from the time the eldest was in his cot, until after the youngest was at school and we continued the practice in school holidays.

The old saying that "Prevention is better than cure" can be applied to many potential conflict points between parents and children. Parents should ensure that when they have promised that something will happen, that it does happen. Always make absolutely sure that you have the right change ready for your child's pocket money – NEVER miss giving it on time.

Conflict can be avoided by giving children notice before the "crunch" comes. If a child is absorbed in playing, it helps to give advance warning that he will have to stop, rather than leaving it till the last moment. The two-minute rule is invaluable. "We need to go out soon, so in a few minutes, I'll come and help you clear your things away" is so much better than an abrupt, "Hurry up, put your things away, we're going out." It gives the child time to adjust to the fact that he has to stop a pleasurable activity. Learning the art of pre-emption is an invaluable parenting tool. If a child's behaviour is becoming a problem, do all you can to make it easier for him to be good. A child can be protected from misbehaving by changing the subject of conversation, by changing the focus of his attention, or by making him laugh. Avoid confrontation if at all possible. When children are really fractious and impossible, get them outside where they can let off steam if you can, or if not, go into another room. If necessary, arrange a special activity or an outing, just to break the pattern. When kids are perpetually naughty, they could be in need of more hugs and more parents' prayers.

When a child is reluctant to do what needs to be done, there can be a quiet discussion to find a compromise, or a patient explanation as to why there can be no compromise. Whenever it is practical, children should be helped to understand the reasons for things especially when they have done something wrong.

In many homes the pressures of juggling the many varied demands of home, work, children and children's activities pose a threat to a calm and peaceful atmosphere. When I was in the position of facing too many demands on my time these were the things that saw me through:

Early Rising: Like many people, I have always drawn great strength from early morning prayer and Bible study. (I use the Christian Science Weekly Bible Lessons.) An hour or so of quiet before the children are up is worth two or even three hours later in the day. I always found it helpful to be dressed myself before I got the children up.

Lists: I'm a great believer in lists and always list jobs to be done. If you work outside the home, make your list of things to do the next day before you go home – it's much easier than doing it when you arrive in the morning. I always sit down on a Sunday evening to plan the menus for the coming week. Just cooking what's planned is so much easier than having to think about it every day and it's easier to shop ahead too.

Plan Ahead: Do jobs earlier instead of later whenever you can, then you don't end up with an almighty last minute rush. It's no good deciding that a job needs to be done, unless you also decide when you will do it.

Set Priorities: Only you can decide what the order of your priorities should be. A top priority for me was and still is, to make time to talk to my family when they need me. If a particular activity is especially important to you, just GO and don't waste time asking yourself, "Can I spare the time?"

Seize Opportunities: I once read a story that went like this: Two friends often played golf together and one morning, the one called at the other's house so they could go together to the club. He arrived early and his friend wasn't ready; he was rummaging round in his desk to find a bill he needed to pay. "I must tidy this desk sometime" he muttered. "Why not do it now?" asked his friend. The man looked startled, Do it now? What a revolutionary idea! But he did. I've found that there are numerous occasions when you can do a job if you just get on with it when the thought comes to you. What does it matter if the time is unconventional?

Eliminate: An old Chinese proverb says, "The wisdom of life consists in the elimination of non essentials." I think of this any time when things get *really* tight and I eliminate like mad!

Family Activities

A good hard look needs to be taken at the amount of time family members spend sitting in front of either of the two small screens that now tend to dominate family activities – the computer and the TV. As the number of small screens have proliferated, so have the number of dysfunctional families – families who have apparently forgotten how to communicate and interact happily with each other.

We will never return to the days when homes were lit by candlelight, nor will we go back to the times when the only entertainment was sitting around a piano listening to one of the ladies singing, but this should not blind us to the fact that today we do have choices. Just as we use electric lights for most purposes, but enjoy candles on certain occasions, even so we may use TV and computers for some of our home entertainment and as sources of information, but we should also include activities where personal involvement is called for. Virtual reality isn't half as interesting as actual reality. Children need to be shown by example that such useful facilities as TVs and computers are wonderful tools to use, but that's what they are – tools – and must remain our servants and not our masters. In America the idea of having a "tubeless week" once a year is gaining ground and one family I know keeps their TV in a corridor where you have to stand to watch, so their kids don't watch too much.

How often we hear today the plaintive wail that "I'm bored" or that teens "have nothing to do". Play with the children in your life – board games, ball games, card games, doing jig-saws or just building with bricks. Games are valuable in teaching children to take turns, to smile when someone else wins and to persist when you don't succeed at the first go. One of the best games for encouraging moral values must be Snakes and Ladders, providing you take the time to study the little pictures. Encourage children to produce their own shows with their friends. They can sing, dance, perform sketches or gymnastic feats, act short stories or do magic tricks and tell jokes. Get children to read and if they belong to the "won't read" brigade, then read to them. Don't let them miss out on the joy of books. Some talented grandparents I know produced really lovely personalised books for each of their grandchildren.

When my eldest grandson was quite little I wanted to help him to understand that things like selfishness do not make you happy, so we devised a game called Happy Town on a huge sheet of thick paper which we put down on the garage floor. The little houses of Happy Town were drawn at the top of the paper and a straight road led up to them. (It had to be straight because it's the "straight and narrow way" which leads to life.) But other roads called disobedience, unkindness and the like turned off the straight road and if you got on to one of those you had to go back to a fuel pump and refill with kindness, obedience etc. before you could proceed on your way. Anti-social behaviour delayed your progress to Happy Town. Our grandson liked the game and some years later it was produced commercially.

Hobbies are a missing element in too many young lives, for hobbies help to develop the qualities of initiative, imagination and self-sufficiency as well as widening one's knowledge. Introduce children to your own hobbies. Do some watercolour painting and the children will want to have a go, do some knitting and they'll want to learn. It is really sad that stamp collecting has gone out of fashion for it was fun, it improved one's knowledge of geography, was good for swaps with your friends and was of more lasting value than collecting football stickers. I have a sneaking sadness too that the days are long gone when little girls sat sewing samplers, for as well as learning dexterity with the needle, samplers taught patience, neatness and accuracy and the end product was something to cherish for ever.

Both boys and girls should always participate in home-making skills like cooking and cleaning. Children who make a contribution to the running of a home – or to the running of a family business – gain in maturity, poise and self-worth. The child who is not expected to contribute to his family is a deprived child. Children love to run errands and to be involved in household activities with cooking being the favourite for most children. Providing duplicates (or triplicates) of things like potato peelers, chopping boards, rolling pins and cutters makes it easier for children to help. Small children are never happier than when they are allowed to make soup, especially if it involves getting vegetables or herbs from the garden and putting them straight into the brew. And what could be more satisfying than making a batch of cakes and then helping to eat them, whilst they are still warm from the oven?

An article I read years ago appealed to me a lot, because it regarded little children in such a positive light. It was called "Mother's Helper" and included this passage: "A mother can always use a helper around the house. She needs someone to match the socks, to watch in the saucepan and call 'It's moving' and to open bottom drawers. When she's driving a mother welcomes knowing when the light has turned green, where the stop signs are, what the speed limit is, what street to turn down to go home."

Children should have their first number lessons from their parents, possibly counting how many stairs to go up and down. Parents can teach the first lessons in reading – and there are excellent videos to help. Geography, history, current affairs and general knowledge can all be learned at home. See that children are acquainted with what's going on in the world. When you go on a trip, show the children where you are going on the map – is it north, south, east or west? As soon as they can, get them to map read.

Letting children help with planting seeds, or better still, have their own patch of garden where fun plants such as sunflowers, marigolds and pumpkins can be grown, nurtures good qualities as well as plants. Walking and cycling are wonderful activities for families to share. Many simple activities are more productive than a day at a theme park and they certainly cost less.

The so-called sophistication of the present generation of children is over-estimated. We have a home movie projector and possess some silent, black and white cartoons which must be some of the earliest and most basic cartoons ever made, yet of all our films, these cartoons are the grandchildren's favourites. (That is, apart from the films we have made ourselves with the children writing the stories and then starring in the film).

It may be a truism that the simpler things in life are best, but providing young children with paper, card (old cereal packets will do), pen, pencil, scissors and selotape can keep them happy for hours and do more than most things to develop initiative, patience and imagination.

One sometimes sees children getting into trouble because there are too many "No-no's". This is sad and can be avoided by providing an environment where children can amuse themselves without damage to themselves or things and then leaving them to it.

Family Rules

At Runnymede, where the Magna Carta was signed, a memorial, given by the American Bar Association, bears this inscription: "To Commemorate Magna Carta symbol of Freedom under Law".

We all cherish freedom, yet freedom for one individual cannot be the right sense of freedom if it is to the detriment of others. If people are to work and live together in harmony, rules are needed. Obeying the rules is what enables us to get the most out of life, whether it is playing football, assembling DIY kits or cooking a gourmet meal. In every family, simple rules are necessary and children need to know them and obey them. When children go to school, there will be school rules, so if they get acquainted with the idea of rules at home, it certainly helps.

A toddler should learn early on the need to say "Please" and "Thank you"- known in many families as the 'magic words'. Children acquire these quite readily when their parents are generous in using them. "Please pick that up" followed always by "Thank you" gives a good parental example. It is even better when children are taught to follow this by naming the person they are speaking to. "Thank you Daddy" or "I'm sorry Mummy" sound really nice. A child can quickly learn that thanks are due when leaving some-one's house, but that strange phrase "Thank you for having me" can surely be improved. Why not "Thank you for the nice time"? These first rules are so easy to learn and enforce, for adults can always withhold something the child wants until the magic word is spoken.

At the dinner table the rules might be: "You must eat at least one mouthful of anything on your plate," "Any item that you chose yourself you must eat," or "You may leave a little on your plate but you must finish your drink." All that is required of the parent is consistency, patience and determination.

Some families have family conferences to agree rules together, so that the children do not feel that rules are just arbitrary regulations imposed by their parents. Rules can be made to avoid particular areas of conflict between siblings and may cover such diverse areas as asking permission before borrowing, returning borrowed items after use, telling secrets in private, leaving the bathroom tidy and cleaning up your own messes. Specific rules are easier to obey than general ones that may leave room for debate. One family where there were endless conflicts had a family conference to try to resolve the problems. They listed the rules that had been hammered out together and posted these rules in a prominent place. After a time, the list was discarded because it had achieved its purpose and one of the children remarked, "We don't need these any more because we're so nice to each other now."

Parents need the moral courage to stick to the rules in their own family, even when their standards are different from those of their neighbours. It is reasonable that visiting children abide by your rules when in your house and that any rules that apply to them are pointed out when they arrive. One mother said "I never argue my rules with my neighbours, I simply say 'I think its best' and leave it at that." Rules are needed for when children are in other people's homes, like not watching videos without their own parent's agreement.

Concern about child abduction makes safety rules imperative. The simplest rule I've heard is this: Children must understand that their parents must ALWAYS know where they are, therefore they must NEVER go anywhere with ANYONE (not even with their grandparents) without checking with their parents first. Children must understand that their parents need to know where to find them if they should be late home. Moreover, it is polite to parents to tell them where they are.

As children become young adults different rules will be needed regarding whether visitors are allowed when parents are out, whether you allow smoking or drinking or whether you will allow an unmarried couple to share a room in your house. I have friends who are extremely tough on this one but find that their views command respect. In one instance, a son threatened to leave home when he was not allowed to sleep with his girlfriend, so his parents said "We're sorry, but we must say 'Goodbye'". He went, but two weeks later returned – minus girlfriend – and apologised. It is sad, however to hear of instances where parents have taken an unyielding stand for the moral high ground even at the price of losing touch with a son or daughter whose marriage has failed, is wary of further commitment and who has fallen prey to current mores.

Although you cannot dictate how your adult children will behave when away from home, you do have the right to say what is and is not permitted when they are in your house. Parents have all the growing years to lead their children in the ways that they feel are right; they eventually have to let them go and trust them to their heavenly Father's guidance.

Note for In-laws

The rules here are simple. Try with all your might to strike a balance between lending a helping hand if required and interfering. Do the former and not the latter. Remember that your son or daughter now has new allegiances and he or she and the new spouse will develop their own life-style. Mind your own business and allow them the space to do their own thing. When grandchildren arrive, do not interfere with the way in which they are being brought up. If you want to drop a word of advice, do it gently and don't take offence if it is not heeded.

Note for Broken Families

If there has been a family break-up, the children have commonly been witnesses to much abuse and acrimony and the one redeeming factor about being with just the one parent, is that things can be expected to be more peaceful. Don't make things harder for the children by using them as bargaining tools and don't try to alienate them from the absent parent.

Criticising the other parent places children in a desperately difficult situation, for they will usually still love both their parents. Remember that, more than any other one thing, children need the parent's time – this is much more valuable than any amount of "guilt money". If a new person comes into your life, realise you will be acting differently when that person is around – you won't be your usual self and this can be hard on your kids, so take things gently for their sakes.

Learning Social Skills

Have you ever noticed the frequency with which a report of a violent crime will include the comment that the criminal was "a loner"? To teach a child how to be a friend is to pave the way for good relationships. The qualifications are set out most succinctly in the saying, "To have a friend, you have to be a friend." In other words you have to be thoughtful of others, treat them as you would like to be treated and be ready to take the first step in making a new friend. A journalist who was leaving for a world tour had a happy approach to meeting new people. He wrote, "Strangers are the friends you haven't yet made."

Looking after "number one" has become a top priority for too many people and advertisements frequently serve to endorse this as a priority, but the truth of the matter is that "a man wrapped up in himself is a very small parcel".

Many thoughtful writers have warned of the dangers to society when "doing your own thing" becomes the motivation of life. All too often people just think about what they can do for themselves instead of what they can do for others, and their children too are allowed to grow up thinking only of themselves. Extreme selfishness is a common characteristic of all children who get into trouble and must be counteracted in order to stop delinquency.

A man who for years suffered on and off from deep depression and suicidal feelings, frankly confessed, "One part of the trouble had been a preoccupation with *my* needs, *my* desires, *my* views, *my* way of doing things. In other words, self-absorption. Facing it squarely, I saw how central this was to so many of my difficulties."

Educating children to consider the needs of others can begin in babyhood by simply sharing their toys. As the child grows, there are many ways in which he can be taught to think of the needs of others, for instance, one family taught their children that when they were introduced to someone new, they should ask themselves, "What can I do for you?" Children can be guided and helped to take the initiative in seeing what needs doing for someone and then doing it. When little children learn to recognise that the urge to do kind things comes from God, it gives them a sense of awe. "

Wow! That was really God telling me to help clear the table?"

Children love to entertain their friends and in Victorian times dolls were used to teach little girls how to keep house and how to have tea parties. Unfortunately it has now become all too commonplace to take children out somewhere for celebrations, instead of having a party at home. Whilst this has some advantages, it can deprive children of the opportunity to play host or hostess; they miss out on the excitement of planning and preparing for a party. Traditional games like hunt the thimble, pinning on the donkey's tail, musical statues, sardines, musical parcel (with forfeits!) and treasure hunts, all gave such simple pleasure and are being forgotten, replaced by going to yet another play area, or a commercial enterprise that supplies food, entertainment and party bags, and every party is the same as every other.

When parents make the time to buck the trend and involve children in organising their own special party, a lot of pleasure is given. One of the best parties I've heard about was one where a ten-year old decided she'd like a formal tea party. Her dad dressed as the butler, an older sister was a waitress and her mother was the cook. The party girl became a duchess for the day and invitations were sent out to "The Duchess's Tea Party." It was such a resounding success that it was still being talked about weeks later.

A simple matter like conversation round the dinner table is part of learning social skills. A survey in America showed that the one thing the majority of successful children had in common was that they came from families where everyone sat down each day to take a meal together. Sometimes a special topic can be discussed and the children can be asked for their opinions on that topic. Eating around the telly is no substitute, just as talking to strangers on the Internet is no substitute for exchanging ideas with real life friends.

Parents need to give a lot of their time to talking constructively with their children and sharing jokes with them. Sharing time together helps children to relate better to others. I've never spoken to the Queen, but I've heard it said that she makes you feel as though you are the one person in the whole world that she'd most like to talk with at that moment. That's the kind of genuine attention that benefits children and gives them an example to follow.

One of the most effective ways of developing social skills is expressed in this poem by Edwin Markham:

They drew a circle that shut me out,
Heretic, rebel, a thing to flout;
But love and I had the wit to win -
We drew a circle that drew them in.

Motives and Reasons

How many times, when a child is asked why he did a thing he shouldn't have done, do we get the reply, "I don't know"? Well, he should know! He should be taught to know why he is doing things. One's motives, whether for good or bad, are the driving force behind every action and it is no wonder that when a person is unaware of his motives that he is working in a moral vacuum, hence the phrase, "mindless violence".

The law says that stealing is wrong, yet everyone would acknowledge that the woman who steals dresses because she is crazy about new clothes, is more deserving of punishment than the man who steals some food to feed his starving children. Both are thieves, but what makes the difference is the motive.

The good man is motivated by unselfishness and thoughtfulness when he helps out a neighbour in trouble; a murderer is motivated by hatred, revenge, sadism or fear when he commits his grisly deed. Cultivating the ability to analyse motives really helps to determine the right course of action and protects one's mental integrity, whereas going along with the crowd weakens it. Learning to analyse one's motives gives the clue to sorting out what is not always black and white, but all too often a shade of grey. Children also need to understand that evil commonly comes in the guise of goodness – for example, tell a lie and you'll get off the hook. Analysis of motives, helps to uncover that subtle disguise and not be tricked by it into doing something that one will regret later.

It is also useful to know that sometimes, in difficult circumstances, the nearest right may lie in choosing between the lesser of two evils, so never berate yourself if you have done your best and then, with the advantage of hindsight, feel you could have done better.

Doing something just because every one is doing it, or to keep up with the Jones's is never the right way to make decisions because these motives are flawed. This is a difficult lesson for children to learn, for overcoming peer pressure is one of the hardest challenges for anyone of school age. This is why moral courage (considered in chapter 4) is such an important component of character.

Bill Gates, presently the richest man in America, must have grown up with a freedom from peer pressure, for when he was quite young, instead of going out to play with the other children, he was in the habit of visiting his school library. The librarian finally gave up suggesting that this persistent little boy should go out with the others and allowed him to help her. She taught him the Dewey Decimal system of book classification, so he could sort returned books, thereby helping to lay the foundation for his very successful career. Examples such as this can be helpful to share with children to encourage them not to be pressured to go along with the crowd, but to develop the habit of independent thinking.

Children should be taught – by example – that the correct basis for decision making is to do something because it is the right thing to do, and to do it irrespective of whether or not it is your best friend at the receiving end. The highest motives are to do what is good and right – we should do good whenever we see a need, irrespective of who is to be the recipient. Children respond very well to this principle and if they are guided to live by it, they will discover the inward peace and satisfaction that correct motivation bestows. Mary Baker Eddy said, and rightly, that right motives, give pinions to thought and strength and freedom to speech and action.

Money Matters

Many children from well-heeled families suffer from their parents' good intentions to provide for their family simply because the parents end up being too busy earning money to spend time with their children. More than any other one thing, children need to have their parents spend time with them, to teach them, to talk with them and to have fun enjoying each other's company. Time spend together when your children are tiny is worth more than any amount of money. Isn't it worth trading holidays abroad for the satisfaction of giving your children the love and attention that will help them develop into well-adjusted adults? Is the child brought to school in a silver Mercedes by parents who have no time to hear him practice reading – and that really happened near where I live – getting a good deal?

One little six-year old who was consistently spoilt by indulgent grandparents, said to me, "I don't need any pocket money – I've got millions of things." That child was, in effect, being deprived – deprived of the pleasure of wanting something, saving for it and feeling a sense of achievement when it was finally purchased. He was also being deprived of the opportunity of learning how to handle money.

Having pocket money and possessing a moneybox initiate a child into the wise use of available resources. Moneyboxes are not in common use today – does their scarcity help to pave the way for the thousands of adults who are unable to pay off their credit card bills?

It gives children a great sense of accomplishment to have a moneybox and a modest amount of pocket money, which they can be reminded to take with them when going out shopping. They should generally be allowed to spend the money just as they choose, with an understanding that Mum has a veto. When the veto is used Mum should explain why a purchase is being disallowed. There is today an increasing awareness of the implications of how we spend our money. More people are investing their money in a manner that suits their ethical concerns and, as consumers, we are becoming more aware of the conditions under which goods are produced and deciding whether we wish to support those methods. As children grow up, they too, can be made aware of where their money is going.

One of the best ideas I've heard of how pocket money for older children should be allocated is the 10 – 20 – 30 – 40 % scheme. In this scheme, 10% of the money is for tithing, 20% is for short term saving, 30% for long term saving and 40% is cash for spending. As soon as the child is mature enough to cope, probably around the age of 13, a clothing allowance can be added to pocket money and this allowance can include all clothes, including school uniform. Clothes shopping can be a real hassle and I chose to withdraw my involvement as soon as possible. Yes, our children sometimes bought clothes we'd rather they didn't wear, but we felt that there were more important areas where we wanted to put a foot down and if they had a free rein on clothes, it was easier to stand firm on matters like what time they were expected in at night.

We sometimes hear the saying, "Money is the root of all evil" but this is a misquotation, for the Bible, where the quotation is found, never says that money is the root of all evil, but that the love of it is, and that is a very different matter. There is nothing wrong with having money, it is a convenient medium of exchange whereby we can express our gratitude for goods or services received and it can enable its possessor to do much good.

The *love* of money for its own sake on the other hand, is at the root of most criminal activity. Drug dealers are so engrossed in their own profits that they care not one whit for the damage they are doing to young lives. Putting profits before people is still an unsavoury aspect of too many big businesses. Love of money detracts from unselfish giving and warps our sense of what constitutes happiness. In the words of Henry Drummond, and the italics are his, "*there is no happiness in having or in getting, but only in giving.*"

The damage that a love of money causes can be seen in post war animal husbandry. Love of money was the motivation for introducing factory farming, and BSE reared its ugly head following the practice of saving money by feeding waste offal to herbivores. Other animal abuses like the genetic engineering of cows to produce unnaturally high milk yields are all done to increase the producers' profits with no compassion for the animals. How can this be right?

Love of money drives some people to work long hours for cash they don't really need and they can end up being more concerned with getting that money, than they are with what the getting of it is doing to the quality of their lives. Having plenty of money is an undoubted asset, but it is not a necessary component for a happy family life, in fact, it can be hard for an affluent family to bring up children with a balanced attitude to money.

A director of a multinational company, and his family, impressed me by the great care they take to see that the children are growing up with a proper sense of the value of money. Just before Easter one year, the family went on a trip to Eurodisney, and both sets of grandparents went along too. They travelled first class on Eurostar and stayed at one of the best hotels. Before they went in to Eurodisney the children were told, "Now understand, you are not to ask for a single thing! No asking for ice creams, no asking for toys. Before we leave, you will be allowed to choose one toy as a souvenir." When the time came to go, the children were told they could choose any toy that was under the equivalent of £5. The little girl soon found something, but the boy was choosier, so his grandma went with him to another shop. The thing he really wanted cost £8. What was Grandma to do? What was a mere £3 when they had spent thousands on the trip? But Grandma was made of stern stuff and wouldn't undermine her son's authority. "I'll tell you what we'll do," she said to her grandson, "I'll pay the extra £3, but if I do, there'll be no Easter egg for you this year." He agreed and grandma stuck to her guns when Easter arrived. She took her little granddaughter to buy an egg, but not the grandson. He understood; he remembered the deal.

The resourcefulness of those with fewer of this world's goods was illustrated by the experiences of a lady I knew who grew up in the years preceding World War II (and also preceding family allowance). She was one of a family of five and lived in a "poor" area of town. Her parents played games with the children, encouraged them in hobbies and good reading and expected all the family to help with jobs around the house. They had no car and took no holidays, but their parents took them to a park each weekend to play games and their mother was always at home when they came in from school. This lady told me, "We may not have had money, but we were richly blessed. We went to Sunday School and what we learnt there and what our parents taught us, gave us a good moral foundation which has stood us in good stead for the rest of our lives." The lady herself and all her siblings grew to be dependable, honest citizens.

Teaching children a balanced attitude towards money can be very challenging, but I've found it helps if children can understand that money only serves as a means to an end. Its not the money a child wants, but the sports bike, the computer game or the new clothes.

Discipline

"If you make clear to the child's thought the right motives for action, and cause him to love them, they will lead him aright: if you educate him to love God, good, and obey the Golden Rule, he will love and obey you without your having to resort to corporeal punishment." So wrote Mary Baker Eddy. Making the right motives clear to a child can be done by example and instruction, but causing a child to love the right motives is a prayer job.

Children need to understand that being naughty brings punishment and being good brings rewards. As with donkeys, the carrot is always better than the stick and if you find you're in the situation where there's too much proverbial – or literal – stick, take this as a sign that it is not the child, but your approach, that needs some adjustment. A little imagination and humour can work wonders when disciplining a child.

A mother and two children had had tea with the grandparents. The nine-year old had been behaving badly. Her father was away, her mother had a lot to do and felt she couldn't cope with the further bad behaviour being threatened by the daughter. ("No I WON'T go straight to bed when we get home".) Grandmother had a sudden inspiration, took the little girl aside and said firmly, "Now stop crying. Would you like a chocolate?" That dried up the tears pretty quickly. "I have a new box of chocolates", continued Grandma, "I will let you choose one if you promise me that you will go to bed immediately you get home – no arguments, no delaying – straight away. We will tell your mummy that I am a good witch and I have put a magic spell on you. You are not to tell *anyone* that you have had a chocolate. Now will you do that?" It worked!

A mother felt that her daughter, who was sometimes reluctant to practice the piano should not be allowed to neglect her musical talent, so a jar of pennies was put near the piano, alongside an empty jar. Every time the daughter practised for half an hour, she could transfer a penny into the empty jar and keep it. That worked too.

Another mother made a star chart for her small son that was comprised of small squares where gold stars were stuck when the child had been good. After so many stars, there would be a "treat" square. Treats varied from having a lollipop to visiting a zoo. This chart provided a useful means of focussing attention on good behaviour and proved to be a great encouragement to do the right thing.

Always remember that you are in control. When a child is small – and even when he's bigger – parents hold all the cards. It is in your power to reward good behaviour and to withhold privileges for bad behaviour. Do not abdicate your absolute control. Mothers who feel in despair over their children's behaviour may feel sometimes inclined to give way to tears. Try your very best not to do this, and whatever you do, don't make a habit of it. On VERY rare occasions, if a mother bursts into tears, it can have an effect greater than any other punishment. I know, because my mother did it just once (I was three and had cut off all my curly hair with some blunt scissors). It was the worse punishment I could have had, because up to that point, I didn't know that grown-ups cried and I was horrified.

When punishment is needed, there are many effective methods that do not involve smacking, like banishment to a cot or bedroom, being deprived of a treat or pocket money being suspended. In some families children have to write lines and one family had a thinking stool where wrongdoers were sent to ponder their misdeeds until repentance set in. Another family made the children write about the good qualities that they had omitted to express.

If all else fails, one may have to resort to corporal punishment, therefore until that happy day when all parents and educators are able to maintain discipline without it, the option to use corporal punishment should be open. A school bully who got six of the best from the headmaster and six more from his dad when he got home was more likely to tone down his behaviour than today's bullies who know their teachers' hands are tied. Banning the cane has served to erode respect for authority, children are not learning to take responsibility for their actions and many children whose behaviour needs restraining are being denied the benefit of the discipline they need with the result that too many of them end up in custody. In the debate about corporal punishment, the difference between a sharp smack and a sadistic beating seems to have been ignored.

From the treatment meted out to convicted criminals to the manner of disciplining children in the home, there has been a failure to recognise that, in the words of the wise woman – Mary Baker Eddy, "Without punishment, sin will multiply." J. Edgar Hoover, when he was head of the American FBI said that many youths are "victims of a society where discipline has been replaced by indulgence. They have been cheated out of a sense of responsibility and a respect for authority." Sadly this is still true today.

All too often, small children are **asked** what they want to do, when they should be **told**. Parents should decide the pattern of a child's life – when he is to go to bed and when he is allowed to get up. Parents should decide what a child should and should not eat. Parents should set the rules and maintain them with a sense of fairness and firmness coupled with the expectation that the child will obey. In this way, children feel secure and are pleasant to be with.

Parents who have raised their children in habits of obedience will find that in due course the child rebels at giving unquestioning obedience, for he or she is growing beyond that stage in his development. This signals the beginning of an important transition from your child being subservient to you, to him becoming your friend and equal. The child frequently will be the first to sense the need for adjustment, but wise parents will not be alarmed, but treat this change with flexibility and tact. In any case, Independence Day is an on-going process, not a sudden finality. I found my understanding that both parent and child will have God as their origin was a special help during this period of transition. Providing the child has been well drilled in listening to and obeying that inner voice, as he matures he will then make wise decisions.

An outstanding educator who had some very succinct comments about discipline was Mary Kimball Morgan, founder of the Principia, now both a school and college in St. Louis, Missouri, U.S.A. Her addresses to the parents of her pupils were outstanding in their penetrating analyses of motives and acts, and laid great stress on the need for proper discipline. The following remarks were included in a presentation she made at a Parents' meeting:

"So many men and women are spoiled in the making. Good material to begin with, they fail to make the most of what they have and are, because of resistance to the discipline necessary to success. Not only is there a resistance to the discipline given by parents and teachers, but there often is little or no attempt at self-discipline. "The parent who loves too much to countenance inaccuracy, insincerity, subterfuge, laziness, frivolity, selfishness and irreverence will reap the fruit of such training in the well-ordered lives of the young men and women who will take their places in the community trained for service to God and man."

That paragraph is the key – love your children enough to discipline them.

The Greatest Gift

The greatest gift that a parent can give a child is an awareness that God loves him and that because God is the divine Mind of all, His guidance is always there in the form of conscience, intuition and inspiration. Prayer is the mental mechanism establishing our connectedness to our divine Mind.

The family that prays together stays together.

Basil Hume, the late Roman Catholic Archbishop of Westminster said that mothers should kneel and pray with their children when they put them to bed. He said that praying makes people more sensitive, adding, "It is very difficult to be a praying person and then go out and be beastly to your neighbour." Those who are sincere about prayer would testify to the truth of that, and I do hope that those who aren't in the habit of praying won't skip this section.

Some parents who teach their children the right way to behave, and teach them to pray, fail to support these directives by their own prayers. Pray each day for your children – pray that they will hear the inward voice of God directing their thoughts and actions; pray that the child's inherent love of goodness will be established, and for the eradication of anything that would obscure that goodness. You can also pray to understand more clearly that God is the only real (i.e. *enduring*) power in your child's consciousness and that evil is transient and has no roots from which to grow. The following anonymous prayer can be a good starting point:

God of wisdom
God of love
teach us to understand

our children
and may they understand us,
that we may learn
from each other.
Make us sensitive,
Make us patient,
make us attentive.
As we grow together
in love
let us grow in awareness
of You,
that we may know
Your blessing
upon us and upon
our children.

As God is unchanging goodness and Love, the purpose of prayer should not be to change God, but rather to awaken us to His presence. In the film *Shadowlands*, C.S. Lewis is depicted as saying, "Prayer doesn't change God. It changes us." That's it in a nutshell and we have to be ready and willing to change in order to be blessed by our prayers and emerge from the shadows of despair and disillusionment into the sunshine of Love.

We are constantly surrounded by angels, God's good thoughts. When a child says he cannot get off to sleep, suggest that he catches angels, in other words, listen to the good thoughts that are there waiting. It is much better than counting sheep; children find it interesting – and it works!

The habit of saying grace before meals is probably the most common form of family prayer and helps to make God relevant. It need not become a bland ritual but can be varied by using favourite Bible verses and by different members of the family saying the grace. A lovely bedtime prayer is to acknowledge God as the originator of all the good that has come to us during that day and to thank Him for that good. This is something very simple for a child to understand, and has a dual purpose:

·   It is a good way of making God meaningful in a young life, for it is always very sad to those who have felt the reality of God's guidance to hear it fobbed off lightly as "You were lucky".
·   Gratitude is one of the most important components of a balanced life and needs constant cultivation. (See chapter 4)

Prayer needs to be honest to be effectual for in Cardinal Hume's words, "People need to learn to distinguish between saying prayers and praying." Most children who are taught a prayer will at times fail to make this distinction and get through the words as quickly as they can. In such cases, I say to them, "That wasn't a prayer, that was a gabble!" They smile sheepishly whilst the need to think about what they say is explained. Prayer does not have to be spoken; we can live our prayers by doing good, but words can help to express our innermost desires, which are the heart of our prayers.

Jesus gave us words for only one prayer – the Lord's Prayer. It is infinitely adaptable and children can learn it by heart when they are quite small.

The Lord's Prayer shows that we should:
·   Approach God as a caring Parent and "hallow" – revere and love – His nature.
·   Listen to God and do His bidding right here, right now.
·   Be ready to forgive others and to ask God's forgiveness for ourselves.
·   Turn to God for deliverance when evil seems to attract us.
·   Live by His rules, use His ever-present spiritual power and give Him credit for helping us.

Apart from the Lord's Prayer, which can be used by all age groups, the nicest prayers for children I have come across are these, both written by Mary Baker Eddy.

FOR LITTLE CHILDREN   FOR BIG CHILDREN

Father-Mother God,   Father-Mother good, lovingly
Loving me, –   Thee I seek, –
Guard me when I sleep;   Patient, meek,
Guide my little feet   Be it slow or fast,
Up to Thee.   In the way Thou hast, –
                            Up to Thee.

The book of Psalms has wonderful prayers that appeal to children. The 23rd and 91st Psalms are good ones to start with. Some families have little papers with Bible verses written on them that the children choose and read each morning before school.

Those who pray are less anxious, less prone to depression and more self-confident. If God is treated as a natural presence within a family and prayer is regarded reverently, children feel more secure, loved and happy. Children appreciate knowing that "There is no spot where God is not".

When I asked a nine-year old boy what God meant to him, he replied thoughtfully, "Well more a friend than anything." All children can be helped to feel that God is truly their best Friend and that their best Friend is always close to them, therefore they are never alone. Prayer helps us to attain and maintain this closeness with God, furthermore, the proclivity to pray is inborn and it is said that there are no atheists on a battlefield, but don't let your children wait for such an extremity to discover this inborn desire.

Wonderful things can happen to small children brought up to have a faith in God's love for them. One of my grandsons, when he was three, had been told to keep away from the part of their garden where the beehives were. He ignored the instruction and had three bee stings on his head. (My son knew it was three stings because he removed them). To everyone's surprise, the little boy suffered no ill effects whatsoever. When his three older cousins sceptically questioned him about what happened, his reply was simply, "God takes care of me." I know too of instances, where children who have been persistently unwell, despite being given medication, have asked their parents, "Please can't we just pray about it?" and recovered remarkably quickly. Parents should bear this in mind when they are unsure what to teach their children about God – give your children the opportunity to grow in faith and you could be pleasantly surprised by the results and your children will always be grateful that you prepared the way for them to receive that greatest of gifts – an awareness of God's love.

Facing Death

A child's first encounter with death is usually through the loss of a pet or of an elderly relative. What should the child be told?

Most people feel instinctively that death is not an end and for this reason refer to someone's "passing" or "passing on" instead of saying that they died. It is certainly more comforting to say to a child. "Grandma has passed on so we can't see her any more," than to say, "Grandma is dead."

I find the analogy of a TV set very helpful in explaining death to children. This world and the next can be likened to two different TV channels – you can switch from one to the other; both appear on the same screen, but you can't fill the screen with both channels at the same time. Therefore I tell children that people haven't gone anywhere else; all that happens is that they have "switched channels" and so are no longer visible to us. An anonymous story uses a different simile and is called – Life is eternal:

Life is eternal

I am standing upon the seashore. A ship at my side spreads her white sails to the morning breeze and starts for the blue ocean. She is an object of beauty and strength and I stand and watch her until at length she hangs like a speck of white cloud just where the sea and the sky come down to mingle with each other. Then someone at my side says "There! She's gone."

Gone where?

Gone from my sight – that is all. She is just as large in mast and hull and spar as she was when she left my side, and just as able to bear her load of living freight to her place of destination. Her diminished size is in me, not in her and just at the moment when someone at my side says,

"There! She's gone." There are other eyes watching her coming and other voices ready to take up the glad shout, "There she comes."

The Easter story tells us that life continues after death and when telling it to children I find it helpful to emphasise that Jesus allowed the crucifixion to happen – he was not powerless in the face of his enemies. We can infer this from the fact that on a previous occasion (see Luke 4:28-30) he did not allow his enemies to take him. Children find this a great comfort and without this point being made, the story can be most distressing for them.

One short sleep past, we wake eternally,
And Death shall be no more: Death, thou shalt die!
                                        John Donne

III. What Would Jesus Do?

When Jesus our great Master came
To teach us in his Father's name,
In every act, in every thought,
He lived the precepts which he taught.
                    Attributed to James Montgomery

WWJD? – What Would Jesus Do? is one of the best questions to ask when seeking to know the right way to act in a certain situation. His precepts for living are outstanding in their wisdom and in their adaptability to varied situations, yet the teachings of Christ are not the sole possession of Christians, for biblical precepts are universal truths. These truths work and it is because they work that Christianity used to be known as "the Way." When people really live in the way Christ taught, the world becomes a better place, but Christianity is not a soft option, it requires much mental discipline. As G.K. Chesterton once said, "The Christian ideal has not been tried and found wanting. It has been found difficult and left untried." It is high time it was tried more consistently, for Jesus' life and work revealed the divinity and high potential inherent in everyone. To behave in the ways that he taught and lived is within the potential of every child and adult. I include here a selection of precepts either quoted directly in Jesus' words, or from those who learnt from Him, and they are all applicable to the upbringing of children.

Turn the Other Cheek

How many little boys have been instructed by their well-meaning parents in words similar to these, "If he hits you, you just hit him back!" These parents say, "I tell him, he must never hit girls, or anyone smaller than him, but he's got to learn to stand up for himself!" Yet the Master Christian, whose understanding of human nature was unsurpassed, gave the opposite instruction – don't retaliate: "Whosoever shall smite thee on thy right cheek, turn to him the other also." (Matthew 5:39)

Jesus was teaching the plain, simple fact that if you have no fear in your heart and refrain from retaliation, you won't be hit again. I have taught infant classes many times not to fight back and if the reply came, "Well my Mummy tells me to hit back," I'd say, "Well try not hitting and see how it works." I never had a child who complained that it didn't work; neither did I ever have a single complaint from a parent.

I talked to one class of five-year olds about fighting and told them that Jesus had told us that the best way to stop a fight is by NOT hitting back. I encouraged the idea that being the one to stop a fight was much cleverer than carrying it on. A few days later, when the children came in after playtime, the toughest little lad in the class swaggered in, came up to me and said so proudly, "He hit me Mrs. Jesper but I didn't hit him back, I was the one who stopped it." To stop the fight had become a sign of strength, not weakness.

This Christian method of stopping a fight is used in the animal kingdom by weaker animals when attacked by a stronger opponent. The weaker animal does not attempt to retaliate, but rolls over on his back to expose his belly or stretched out neck; in other words, he puts himself at the mercy of the other animal who never takes advantage of the situation. This is how the weaker animal protects himself when he wouldn't stand a chance in a fight. The important thing is that this be **done without fear.**

In *The Naked Ape* Desmond Morris writes, "Special submissive postures have been evolved which automatically appease a dominant animal and inhibit its attack" and in *Animal Societies from the Bee to the Gorilla* we read, "This is the place to take notice of the curious submissive behaviour which is found in all animals pursued by a despot. An attacked mouse turns and rises on its hind legs to expose its vulnerable belly; under the same circumstances a wolf offers its throat, and the attack stops at once. It is a clear case of a well-characterised posture and not an accidental one."

Konrad Lorenz in his book *King Solomon's Ring* in commenting on this behaviour in animals, says, "I at least have extracted from it a new and deeper understanding of a wonderful and often misunderstood saying from the Gospel which hitherto had only awakened in me feelings of strong opposition. A wolf has enlightened me: not so that your enemy may strike you again do you turn the other cheek toward him, but to make him unable to do it."

In early childhood, this will be fearlessly accepted and the child will gain early assurance of its practicality.

This precept can also be applied to verbal confrontations. Keep silent instead of aiming to get one up or to win certain arguments. Salesmen are aware of the need to do this when approaching prospective customers and there is a saying amongst salesman to beware of winning the argument and losing the sale. How much more care we should take to turn the other cheek instead of picking a fight with one of the family when the stakes are even higher.

There is no fear in love; but perfect love casteth out fear.

I John 4:18

Bless them that curse you

This is a step further than turning the other cheek, for it demands a positive response to provocation, condemnation, bullying, intimidation, violence or hatred in any of its myriad forms. As with turning the other cheek, it is an effective tactic for disarming evil. When one hears tales of dreadful rows between neighbours, one thinks of what a difference it would make if one of the warring factions were to present the other with a home-made pie straight from the oven.

The great value of children learning this precept for living is that it empowers them when they feel victimised, and when a victim is empowered, he's no longer a victim – he's in charge of the situation, or you can say that he is lifted out of the situation because he's obeying a higher law. I've found that the simplest way of encouraging children to follow this path of blessing is this: This person who has behaved badly to you, shouldn't have behaved in that way, should he? (The child will always agree). So if he shouldn't have behaved in that way, he needs help in doing better. You can show him a better way by doing something good for him. If you can't immediately find something good to do, then you can at least think kindly about him.

A girl who endured a bad patch of being bullied at school was told to persist in thinking about those who were responsible, "Despite what you say or do, I love you." She didn't find this easy (remember, Christianity isn't a soft option) but she was obedient and in a short while the bullies responded to her unspoken blessing upon them and friendly relations were restored. Then a dose of forgiveness is also required.

Blessed are the peacemakers: for they shall be called the children of God.   Matthew 5:9

Go to Your Brother

"If thy brother shall trespass against thee," said Jesus, "go and tell him his fault between thee and him alone." (Matthew 18:15). It takes moral courage to obey this instruction, but it is undoubtedly the best approach. It is always better to have a quiet word with the offending party than to go complaining to other people.

At one time when we were on holiday at a large campsite, there was a great deal of noise one night from a group of young adults. Several campers were unable to sleep and were voicing their annoyance the following morning and one man threatened to report the young people to the camp warden. Remembering Jesus' instruction on how to treat such situations, I sought an opportunity instead to speak with two of the group. I had a friendly chat, saying that I thought they should know that a number of people had been put out last night because their sleep had been disturbed. Consternation appeared on their faces. "I thought perhaps you'd rather I told you, because I wouldn't like to see you get into any trouble." I said. They then relaxed a bit, thanked me for telling them and assured me they wouldn't do it again. They kept their word and there were no more rowdy nights.

A friend of mine told me of trouble they had had at her church, due to repeated instances of graffiti being written on a side wall. One day, my friend called in at the church at a time when normally no-one was there. Whilst she was inside, she heard voices outside, so she went out and found a group of teenagers, one of whom was writing on the wall. My friend remained perfectly calm and explained to the boys that their church meant a lot to the members and they did not like to have it spoilt by graffiti. She further said that she did not want to get them into trouble and that if they would give her their word that they would not do it again, she would let the matter drop. She then insisted that each of them spoke in turn to give her their word that they would not write on the walls any more and each of them did. A little later she passed the boys outside a shop. "Now you'll remember to keep your word, won't you" she said as she went by the group, who meekly assented. That was the end of the graffiti.

The advantage of "going to your brother" is that it helps to heal, rather than inflame, hurt feelings, and therefore is really effective in getting the best response. All situations might not be resolved as readily as these ones were and Jesus knew this too, for he gave follow up instructions for dealing with more stubborn cases by getting some back-up for a repeat visit. "But if he shall not listen to you, take one or two others with you so that everything that is said may have the support of two or three witnesses." (Matthew 18:16, J.B. Phillips translation).

Obeying this rule stops children telling tales. "If you need to tell someone about it, its ————— you should speak to. He's the one who did it". It is excellent training in moral courage for a child to face up to telling another child to stop what he is doing. We found in our family that a good rule for judging if the matter should be taken further is: is someone hurt? (apart from feelings); is anything damaged?

If he shall hear thee, thou hast gained thy brother.

Matthew 18:15

Magnify Good

St. Paul wrote to the Christians in Philippi, "Finally, brethren, whatsoever things are true, whatsoever things are honest, whatsoever things are just, whatsoever things are pure, whatsoever things are lovely, whatsoever things are of good report; if there be any virtue, and if there be any praise, think on these things." (Phillippians 4:8) When I was teaching five-year olds, we wrote Paul's words in the front of a large book which detailed the good qualities of everyone in the class. The children thought of something good to say about each member of the class – they were encouraged to make them varied – and then every child drew a self-portrait to accompany the text. We got comments like, "Nigel likes to find out how things work," and "Debbie is very helpful" etc. The children loved it and the book was popular with parents on Open Day – I guess they all enjoyed reading something nice about their child! A student doing teacher training used a similar idea in a top junior class and at the end of the practice she gave each child a certificate for something the child had achieved whilst she had been there. The children were really thrilled to take these certificates home.

The head of a school for teenage girls excluded from regular schooling told me that he felt the great importance of always being on the lookout for something positive to say about his pupils, for these girls, even more than others, needed to build their self-esteem. To magnify good is an excellent practice in the home as well as providing good material for school projects. A single mother who was finding the going tough, put up a notice in the kitchen where she and her daughters wrote down any good thing that had happened that day. Initially she was the only one to contribute, but after a few days, the girls began to add their own contributions and it really lightened the load. The media so often emphasise bad news and place so much emphasis on the sensational that something needs to be done to see that one doesn't get overwhelmed by the negative. We can remind ourselves that good is more prevalent than evil; law would be unenforceable if this were not the case.

Leonardo Da Vinci once said "Reprove your friend in secret and praise him openly," and this is a good hint to adults, on how to act towards their children – and also to their partners. Parading a child's faults and misdeeds before others merely magnifies those very faults that you should be seeking to minimise and eradicate. This does not mean that children should not be corrected – far from it! It relates rather to the question of emphasis. Always magnify good if you want to see it grow, make much of a child's successes and help him gently, firmly but privately over his failures. If a child was helping with a job in the house and spills something, let the mess be quietly cleaned up (child helping) and when the rest of the family are there, mention the helpfulness but say nothing of the spill.

When parents have this approach, their children learn to magnify the good and to minimise the not so good. An example of this happened in the conversation a little boy had with his friend "My sister is a nuisance to me" said the friend. "Well my sister isn't a nuisance to me," was the little boy's reply. Afterwards he confided to his Mum, "Even if she is a nuisance sometimes, Mum, I wasn't going to say so."

A teenage girl used the dictum of magnifying good when a new girl moved into her neighbourhood and found it hard to make friends. She started to talk to the newcomer, looked for her good qualities and told the other kids how nice she was. This helped the new girl to gain a circle of friends.

Looking for what is good is extremely helpful in dealing with all human relationship problems. At one time my daughter was being taught by a retired teacher who had stepped in to help at her school when they were short of staff. The teacher was obviously finding it difficult to teach very young children and most of them had decided they disliked her. My daughter was upset because she felt the teacher had been unfair to her, and she didn't want to go to school. So I gave her the job of finding one good thing about the teacher. This appealed to her and she agreed to try. That afternoon, my daughter was really happy when she came home, for she had not only found one thing, but three! The teacher could sing sweetly, she told stories well and she was tidy. This stopped the unhappiness, and appeared to pave the way for a general improvement in the atmosphere in the classroom.

There are many other applications of this mental exercise – it can help a shy child to turn their thoughts to others instead of focussing on themselves and brothers and sisters can be asked to tell their parents something good about each other at the end of the day.

Remember that thou magnify his work, which men behold.

Job 36:24

Resist the Devil

What is this devil that we need to resist? The devil is a concept that draws forth many conflicting opinions and definitions, but there are some straightforward answers that are quite simple for children to understand.

First of all, I think everyone would agree that the devil stands for something evil. Now little children like to play around with words. They warm to the idea that if you put an extra "o" into "God", you have "good". Similarly they like to know that "devil" is "evil" with a "d" in front. Jesus himself said that the devil is an enemy. He also said "He is a liar" and I've found that this is an excellent starting point for children of all ages, for when you know that something is a lie, it no longer fools you. However this does not imply that the devil is something to be ignored. It is not a case like that of the three little monkeys, See no evil, Hear no evil and Speak no evil. We need to face up to evil and resist it, which is what this precept is saying. Older children can also be taught that the word "devil" comes from the same root as the name of that toy that is tossed around on a string – the diablo – with its meaning "to throw across". If something is being thrown at you, then you need to shield yourself from it – to put up a resistance, as Jesus' brother James instructed, "Resist the devil and he will flee from you". This resistance is not a physical one; it is a mental demand.

Here is a true story, which tells about how a boy put this biblical precept to good use. Let's call him Dave and the boy he met we'll call Nathan.

When Dave's parents told him they were moving to a new city, his first thought was, "Cool, there might be a boy living right next door" and sure enough when they arrived at their new home Dave saw a boy about his size in the garden of a nearby house.

"There is my friend," he thought, and he waved, but the boy didn't wave back.

The next day when Dave passed the house where the other boy lived, he felt two sharp thumps on his back. He turned round and there stood Nathan with a scowl on his face and his fists doubled up.

"Go back to the corner!" he ordered. "No one walks up here unless I say so." Dave sadly walked back to the corner and walked home another way.

Dave really tried to be friendly to Nathan but without success, then one day he remembered that he had been taught, "Resist the devil, and he will flee from you." Dave knew that this meant facing up to trouble and not running away from it as he had been doing. He also saw that he was not being a good friend to Nathan if he allowed him to bully him and get away with it. So he decided not to take the long way home again.

The following day as Dave approached Nathan's house, Nathan was standing in the middle of the road, with his fists clenched, but this time Dave walked right up to him and suddenly knew what to say. He said, "Why hit your friend?"

"I don't have any friends," said Nathan.

"Yes, you do," said Dave, "I'm your friend."

This change of tack just disarmed the bully and from that day on the two boys became firm friends. In another instance, an older lad, James, was intimidating a younger boy, Sam. Sam discovered that James liked playing marbles, but kept this quiet because marbles weren't cool amongst his set, so when Sam won some marbles, he saw an opportunity to change this unhappy situation and he presented the marbles to James.

"I won these for you," he announced.

"Really?" James didn't quite know how to respond but he accepted the marbles and that was the end of the intimidation and these boys too became friends.

Examples like these confirm that the so-called victims of bullying actually have it in their own power to overturn threatening situations. If only more boys – and girls too – could understand that they can resist evil and learn the confidence that it will flee from them, what a help this would be.

> For the weapons of our warfare are not carnal, but mighty through
> God to the pulling down of strong holds.   II Corinthians 10:4

Shutting the Door

In his Sermon on the Mount, Jesus spoke of the need to "shut your door" when you pray. Everyone has a door in their thinking and needs to keep that door open to good impulses but closed to suggestions of evil. When the "door" is guarded and only the thoughts that one wants to see manifested in productive actions are allowed to enter, lives run more smoothly.

An outstanding example of refusing to admit evil into one's thoughts, and the benefits that this brings, is given in a little book called *The Ultimate Freedom* which tells the experiences of the author, John Wyndham, in a Japanese prisoner of war camp in World War II. Wyndham was faced with the likelihood of execution because of incriminating documents found in his possession. In his desperate situation, he prayed and was given the message: CONTROL THOUGHT. He writes,

> From that moment, fearful suggestions, resentful suggestions,
> hateful suggestions were barred from entering consciousness.
> When they came, and they came daily, hourly, and sometimes
> moment by moment, I absolutely refused to let them in. . . . With
> a rusty old nail, I scratched the letters 'CT' on the wall of my cell
> as a constant reminder to control thought.

He goes on to say that his changed thought had an immediate effect on him both mentally and physically. He was not executed, and he developed a constructive relationship with his captors.

Children respond well to the idea of a door to guard their thinking. A friend of mine evolved a little game on this theme and used it with a young Sunday School class. She obtained a commissionaire's cap and the child who wore it was stationed by the door. The other children spoke either a good thought or a bad thought and the commissionaire only admitted good thoughts; the others were barred. The children loved it and remembered the lesson it taught them. It is a game that could well be played in any playgroup or infants' school.

When brothers and sisters rub each other up the wrong way or when school friends fall out, it is an eye-opener for them to learn that other people do not have the power to control how one thinks or feels. "He really annoys me," said a young lady of my acquaintance, speaking about her brother. "No, he can't do that," I assured her, "Whatever he does cannot affect you unless *you let it*. Just don't let it. If he does things he shouldn't do, that's his problem. Why allow it to upset you?"

Wrong impulses should be dealt with as foreign to a child's God-given thinking and, on that basis, excluded from his consciousness. It is a most helpful thing for any child to be taught that bad thoughts are not really his thoughts. A simple way of making this plain to a small child who does something wrong is to say to him, "That's not James, James is a good boy."

This sentiment is echoed in the following statement by John Curton Collins, "We are no more responsible for the evil thoughts that pass through our minds than a scarecrow for the birds which fly over the seed plot he has to guard; the sole responsibility in each case is to prevent them from settling."

If a child is naughty, remember the scarecrow and the birds, and when correcting him, mentally and verbally separate the child from the naughtiness. If your rebuke brings forth the wail, "You don't love me any more" the reply might be, "Yes, I love you very much, but I don't love that naughtiness – so let's finish with it shall we?" Naughtiness isn't the child, it is an evil thought he has allowed to alight in his thinking. It is a case of you and the child ganging up together against the naughtiness – not you and the child opposing each other.

The Dalai Lama of Tibet wrote, "I remind myself that it is the actions of human beings rather than human beings themselves that make them my enemy." A number of writers have written of "separating the sin from the sinner" which isn't entirely an accurate way of stating the case, for if the sin is separated from the sinner, would he still be a sinner? Haven't we all, at some time or other, let slip some thoughtless words and the minute they were out of our mouth, wished we'd not uttered them? At the very moment when we gave the outward appearance of being thoughtless or unkind, we had already disassociated ourselves from what we said and were definitely not the uncaring person we appeared to be. We'd be grateful if someone made allowances for us and we should always be ready to do the same for our children.

Mary Baker Eddy wrote,

You must control evil thoughts in the first instance, or they will control you in the second.

This is something that children can learn to prove for themselves and it generally appeals to them for they like the idea of being in control.

A little boy was once reprimanded for hitting a little girl, but soon afterwards, was doing it again. He was then told that those thoughts that said, "Hit her," weren't his thoughts and he should send them away. This did the trick and the little boy was finally quite triumphant. "Those naughty thoughts kept coming," he said, "but I said 'Go away, naughty thoughts,' and I didn't hit her."

Now if I do that I would not, it is no more I that do it, but sin that dwelleth in me.   Romans 7:20

Giving or Getting?

A young teenager was fed up with being required to go to Sunday School and felt she wasn't learning much anyway. Her parents suggested that she speak to a family friend about the situation, so she did. "I'm not getting anything out of Sunday School," she whined to the friend. He looked at her kindly and asked "*Getting*? What are you *giving*?" This changed the girl's attitude completely and she then began both to enjoy and benefit from the lessons, thus proving the truth of Jesus' words, "Give and it shall be given unto you." (Luke 6:38)

When Christmas or birthdays come around, children's thoughts are usually focussed on what they are going to get, an attitude which is reinforced by kindly adults who never fail to enquire, "What are you getting for Christmas?" This attitude concerned me, for albeit kindly meant, it does encourage selfishness, so I started a practice with my own children, which was continued with my grandchildren, which helped them to think instead, "What am I *giving* for Christmas?" I used to take each one (individually) out shopping to buy small Christmas presents for the rest of the family. They saved some pocket money, which I supplemented, and after the shopping we came back to our house for a gift wrapping session which was great fun! But their greatest joy was and still is, in giving out the presents on Christmas Day and seeing the response from the recipients. I found that children are very good at choosing appropriate gifts even with a modest budget.

In addition to learning to give *things*, there is also the more important question of cultivating an *attitude* of giving, as illustrated in this little story:

"When my sisters, my brother, and I were little, our mom (it is an American story) would call out as we left the house on our way to a party, 'Give a good time!'

"Why didn't she say '*Have* a good time' like everybody else? Because my mom said it was important that we learn to think about other people and how to make *them* happy, rather than just thinking about ourselves.

"So when our mom said '*Give* a good time,' we knew she wanted us to express love toward everybody at the party and not worry about how we looked, whether people would include us in their groups, or whether we would be popular."

The story goes on to tell how at one particular party, the writer won so many prizes that her friend's mother suggested that she share out her prizes with the other children. She continued:

"At first it seemed a little hard to give away the prizes I had won fair and square. But I knew deep down inside that sharing my prizes would be obeying my mom's words to 'give a good time.' I went home with only one prize, but I had the satisfaction of knowing I had done my best in more ways than one.

"At this party I learned a lesson I have never forgotten: that in giving up a few material prizes, I had won a spiritual treasure that could never be taken away from me. That day I saw very clearly that unselfishness blesses the giver as well as the receiver."

It is more blessed to give than to receive.   Acts 20:35

The Golden Rule

We are accustomed to believing that all educational reforms cost a lot of money, but there is one educational reform that would cost no money at all. It is to have a programme right from nursery school through to university level that teaches the most valuable moral instruction that has ever been given on how to act – the Golden Rule.

Treat others as you would like them to treat you.

Such a programme would preserve and develop each child's moral potential and help him to find avenues to use his innate kindness.

The Golden Rule is adaptable to any situation or circumstance and is the basis of all good laws. Every rule in every school is based on the need to think of *others* and to act in a thoughtful manner towards them. Before taking action, try putting yourself in the other fellow's shoes and ask yourself, "Would I like to be treated in this way?" If the answer is "No!" then don't do it. It's that simple! If you don't already use this rule to guide you, try it out and see how well it works.

Taking children out in the car offers many opportunities for explaining how we use the Golden Rule: We can let cars out of side roads if there is a long queue of traffic, we can help drivers who are overtaking by keeping well to the side, we wait to let pedestrians go across crossings, and when we park, we can make sure we don't make it hard for other cars to get out.

The Golden Rule is incorporated in the teachings of every major world religion except Hinduism, which has no rules or creeds, therefore there should be no problem in its teaching and implementation in a multicultural society. When applied, it can be proved to be true and as it doesn't mention God, it should also be acceptable to those with no religion.

Here are the differing versions of the Golden Rule:

CHRISTIANITY
All things whatsoever ye would that men should do to you, do ye even so to them.

BRAHMANISM
This is the sum of duty. Do naught unto others which would cause you pain if done to you.

BUDDHISM
Hurt not others in ways that you yourself would find hurtful.

CONFUCIANISM
Is there one maxim that ought to be acted upon throughout one's whole life? Surely it is the maxim of loving-kindness: Do not unto others what you would not have them do unto you.

ISLAM
No one of you is a believer until he desires for his brother that which he desires for himself.

JUDAISM
What is hateful to you, do not to your fellow man. That is the entire law; all the rest is commentary.

TAOISM
Regard your neighbour's gain as your own gain, and your neighbour's loss as your own loss.

ZOROASTRIANISM
That nature alone is good which refrains from doing unto another whatsoever is not good for itself.

The infinitely adaptable Golden Rule can be applied to every tricky relationship situation that comes along. Do those who are prepared to conceive babies late in life, by artificial means, or those who want to clone humans, consider the Golden Rule? Do they put themselves in the position of the planned child and ask, "Would I like to be in the situation of having a mother old enough to be my grandmother – a mother who will not be around to see her grandchildren grow up?" "Would I like to be conceived as the result of a genetic experiment?"

Children should be taught the Golden Rule by heart, then they will not forget it. Once you are in the habit of remembering the Golden Rule and applying it, you come to appreciate why its called Golden; its so useful. With practice, it becomes your normal way of life.

Here's a true story that can be told to children as an example of using the Golden Rule. Its about a girl called Sally.

There was a new girl in Sally's class at school, named Emily. Everyone in the class turned to look at Emily when she came in and Sally could see that Emily didn't look comfortable. One boy nudged his friend and mumbled something Emily couldn't hear, and then they both laughed loudly. She slid down in her seat, and wished that she could be back in her old school.

Sally could see that the new girl wasn't happy and it disturbed her but she decided that it was none of her business. "I suppose somebody will be her friend," she thought.

Then it was time for break. Boys and girls stood in the playground in small groups talking to their friends and Sally noticed that Emily didn't like to come out.

Just at that moment a group of girls from the other side of the playground shouted, "Sally, come over here! We need you in our team."

She looked at Emily and then at her friends, "Can Emily play?"

"No!" they shouted, "We just want you." Emily heard the answer and turned away. Sally stood still, looking from one to the other. Suddenly she remembered that she had been taught the Golden Rule: "Do unto others as you would have them do unto you."

"I wouldn't like someone to leave me alone and not let me play," she admitted to herself. "I can't do that to Emily."

So she took Emily by the hand and led her over to where her friends were. Then someone said, "Okay, she can play, but hurry up or break will be over before we even get started."

Imagine what a change could come over our schools if they really focussed on teaching the Golden Rule and helped children to implement it. It has the potential to eliminate all the cruelty which children all too often inflict on other children.

When they are used to living by the Golden Rule, children can also be introduced to the Diamond Rule – "Think about others as you would have them think about you".

.... be ye doers of the word and not hearers only, deceiving your own selves.   James 1:22

The Golden Rule, together with three other precepts included here, is incorporated into Jesus' Sermon on the Mount as recorded in Matthew's Gospel, chapters 5-7. The whole Sermon, is the most rewarding study to teach children practical ways to make relations with others go more smoothly.

IV. The Antidotes to the Anti-Social

The basic cause of crime is lack of religious instruction.

Father Flanagan

For we wrestle not against flesh and blood, but against . . . the rulers of the darkness of this world. . . . "   Ephesians 6:12

A prison chaplain was in a prison one day when he observed a warder treating one of the inmates in an unfair manner. "Did you have a Christian upbringing?" he asked the warder, who grudgingly replied that he supposed he did. "Well that guy there (indicating the prisoner) probably didn't. Don't you think you should make some allowance for that?"

A Christian upbringing should awaken the seed of goodness implanted within our being which makes us incapable of wicked deeds. As the Apostle John wrote in a letter, "Whosoever is born of God doth not commit sin; for his seed remaineth in him: and he cannot sin, because he is born of God." (I John 3:9) The great need of delinquents is to experience this awakening. The decline in religious instruction means that many young criminals have not only been brought up by adults devoid of any moral or religious anchor, but in addition have been constantly exposed to an amoral media.

In the 1960s, two books were published which gave remarkable accounts of Christian work amongst violent youth gangs in America and particularly in New York City. One was *The Cross and the Switchblade* by David Wilkerson, and the other, *Run Baby Run* was the story told by Wilkerson's most notable convert, Nicky Cruz. That Nicky Cruz, "the most feared gang leader in Brooklyn" (his words) experienced a complete change from being a ruthless gangster to becoming a committed Christian, must be one of the greatest testimonies in our time to the power of prayer to arouse a desire for repentance.

How many disruptive children are merely craving love and attention? How many disturbed children are desperately in need of understanding? Answer: ALL OF THEM. Few children in trouble have ever been successful at anything, except irritating their parents and teachers. They are frequently below average in their schoolwork and have poor reading ability (aggravated by the fact that they commonly speak badly). They are immature, extremely selfish and have difficulty in establishing normal social relationships. Therefore they seek solace in belonging to a gang or in promiscuity. True satisfaction and inner joy are unknown to these children and they desperately need help in gaining self-worth. Jesus spoke of the need to "love another as yourself" yet the significance of the "as yourself" bit is commonly glossed over; yet you cannot truly love another until you feel really comfortable with yourself.

At the root of all the sad stories we hear about youths in trouble, lie polluted minds, lost opportunities to develop good qualities and ignorance of what constitutes happiness. Confusion over what really constitutes happiness and satisfaction is at the root of vandalism, arson and a tremendous amount of petty crime. A deeply tragic event that occurred within a few miles from where I live illustrated this clearly. A thirteen-year old girl took an overdose of sleeping pills after suffering many cruel taunts about being overweight. A gang of youths had thrown food at her house, but after the suicide, one of them said, "It seemed fun at the time, but its different now."

It took the shock of that poor girl's death to awaken the gang who had previously thought it was fun to throw eggs and margarine at a house wall, to the realisation that their sense of fun had been an illusion.

There is no real fun in being naughty.

The key word here is **real**. Many people, like the youths who threw the food, seem to get a kick out of doing unruly things and believe they enjoy vandalising other people's property. They need to learn that this is not enduring pleasure for its basis is flawed and deep in their hearts no-one truly wants to be bad. Children should have it spelled out to them that "There is no real fun in being naughty."

I have always had reservations about the American Declaration of Independence with its inclusion of "the pursuit of happiness" as one of man's inalienable rights. We do have a right to be happy, but to pursue it for its own sake is not the way in which it is attained – I find the manner of its attainment is best expressed in these two sayings: "Happiness is a perfume you cannot pour on others without getting a few drops yourself" and "Happiness consists in being and in doing good."

Children love to be praised and praise for being good can focus on the satisfaction it gave. Conversely, if a child has been reprimanded for doing something stupid, then it can be made clear that there was really no fun in what he did.

The long-term solution to today's moral ills begins in the home, the playgroup and the nursery school. A whole-hearted national effort in homes, playgroups, nurseries and schools, to teach that there is no real pleasure in sin would effectively reduce our level of crime. Measures like making cars and mobile phones technically harder to steal may effect a short-term lessening of one type of crime, but it does nothing to address the root cause of the problem.

If anti-social behaviour is to be eradicated, the minds of children must be emptied of anti-social thoughts and filled instead with constructive thoughts, or better still, their thoughts should be kept pure in the first place. They must be taught how to protect their mental integrity both against mental domination by others and against the desire to dominate or control others. Much mischief is wrought in this world when the right balance between individuals is eroded by one individual having the desire to dominate another. This desire ruins marriages, friendships and family relationships; it causes criminal activity and at its most pernicious, starts wars. This destructive mental attitude can be effectively nipped in the bud by teaching children to have consideration for others by developing the qualities of kindness, gratitude, gentleness, restraint and generosity.

All bad behaviour involves a failure to exercise a good quality, for disobedient, aggressive and violent actions arise from disobedient, aggressive and violent thoughts. Rudeness comes from a failure to exercise politeness, greed from a failure to exercise moderation etc.

As children learn to overcome disobedient impulses in simple ways in their early years, they will not have to face aggressive or violent impulses in later years, for the foundations of these will have been undermined. Children have a great need to think of themselves as good and need to understand that there is an obligation for them to show this goodness.

The beneficial effect of using good qualities was brought home to a group of schoolgirls who had become victims to bullying. When the school's normal anti-bullying procedures failed to make any impression, the Principal spoke to the girls who were being bullied. She asked them to write down how the bullying made them feel and they wrote down things like, "Humiliated, frightened, insecure" etc. The Principal then had the girls write down the opposites to each of the qualities they had listed, such as confident, secure and serene. They were then told to put these positive qualities into practice. As they gained more confidence in doing this they were no longer picked on; they were learning instead how they could refuse to be victims.

Our qualities define what sort of people we are, they pervade our homes and colour our communities. The qualities we express define our individualities and the qualities expressed by others either attract or repel us. Good qualities are the building blocks of character and they open the way for us to feel at one with that higher power; they help in the development of intuition, inspiration and conscience. Excellence is measured in qualities.

A highly regarded independent school in the south of England runs a two year cycle of selected qualities aimed at bringing out the best that is within their pupils who are taught to analyse the qualities. Co-operation for instance was broken down into teamwork, team building, leadership, relationships, participation and readiness to compromise. Wisdom was analysed as maturity, knowledge, judgement, detachment, understanding and logical reasoning.

Analysing qualities makes it easier to work at polishing one facet of our nature at a time. You might concentrate for a day on being gentle, thoughtful or patient and continue until you felt you had established that quality in your thoughts. We do not really know the meaning of a particular quality unless we are exercising that quality, for example, "He doesn't know the meaning of honesty" implies that he is dishonest.

In his Sermon on the Mount, Jesus gave an instruction that relates to qualities. He said, "Be ye therefore perfect, even as your father in heaven is perfect" (Matthew 5:48). Perfect means, "having all the qualities requisite to its nature." This does not imply that we should all be alike, for it is in the infinite variations between peoples that we glimpse something of the infinite goodness and variety of God. It's not enough to wish that your children have more good qualities; what you need to do is to see that the qualities they need to behave well are right there for them, and to pray that their Father-Mother God will open their hearts, as well as your own, to know that it is their true nature to express good qualities.

Good qualities are not personal possessions, but spiritual endowments and need to be cultivated in young children as assiduously as a gardener protects tender seedlings. Exposure to qualities that are the reverse of the ones we want to cultivate stunt the growth of goodness and virtue. Children need careful protection from such destructive qualities as callousness, hatred, or sadism, which can only have a desensitising effect. The exercise of good qualities necessarily means letting go of their opposites. Every day parents and teachers should nurture and nourish good qualities and reinforce them by their own examples so that they become habitual. Children should learn the names of good qualities as well as how to live them.

There is no doubt about which quality should head the list.

Moral Courage

The year was 1932 and two schoolteachers sat on the top of a London bus. They were partners about to start a boys' preparatory school and were on their way to visit the printers to finalise their prospectus, but there was still one detail to be worked out. They had not decided on a motto for the school. "Which good quality did a boy most need?" they asked each other. They finally agreed that it was moral courage, and pondered how to incorporate moral courage into a simple phrase for their motto.

One of the teachers, Guy Snape, wrote later, "The answer was obvious –

the words spoken by the angel to Daniel (Daniel 10:19) 'O man greatly beloved, fear not; peace be unto thee, be strong, yea, be strong.' So 'Be strong' became our motto. We like to think of our boys going out into the world feeling themselves greatly beloved by God, unafraid, at peace with themselves and their neighbours, and spiritually strong."

At the start of the 21st century moral courage, the antidote to that peer pressure which lures youngsters into anti-social ways, is still the most valuable quality for all young people, for moral courage fosters a robust state of mind that does its own thinking. The morally courageous develop thought habits that are untouched by the taunts of the morally weak, just as the non-smoker is not tempted by advertisements for cigarettes. They have what can be described as a solid silver mentality. As solid silver cannot be magnetised, so the morally courageous are impervious to false attraction.

Moral courage stands for integrity of thought, for doing the right thing – no matter what, and helping others to do the right thing by a kind word or example; it is standing firm for what is right and not budging from that, irrespective of what anybody else thinks or says; it is doing your own thinking instead of letting others do it for you. It is having mental strength. Moral courage for kids is not joining in when your friends all pick on a timid child, it's refusing to be cowed if you are the one being picked on, it's knowing that "Sticks and stones may break my bones, but words can never hurt me." Moral courage for teens is not joining in the chorus that says "cool" to a real or fictional case of brutality; it is being the first to say "No" when a wrong course of action is being proposed and sticking to it, no matter what your friends say. For parents moral courage means sticking to your guns and raising your children in ways that you believe to be right and not bowing down to the way your children's friends' parents are bringing up their children. For everyone, moral courage is not yielding your mentality to other people's opinions – it is keeping the "house" of your consciousness built on "the rock" of what you know to be right.

> Therefore whosoever heareth these sayings of mine, and doeth them,
> I will liken him unto a wise man, which built his house upon a rock:
> And the rain descended, and the floods came, and the winds blew, and
> beat upon that house; and it fell not: for it was founded upon a rock.
> Matthew 7:24,25

Many parents find it a great challenge to teach their children moral courage for they are reluctant to make their children feel different from their friends. They say things like, "Everybody will laugh at you if you do that" instead of helping children to face up to what to do if "everybody" does laugh. It is sad that many youngsters become teenagers without even knowing what moral courage is and not knowing that you don't have to live your life by someone else's book.

The current vogue for "doing your own thing" can be turned to useful advantage in helping the development of moral courage and children should be encouraged to value their own individuality. It can help children if their parents are one jump ahead of tricky situations that they will have to face and discuss with them what they should do. Being forewarned is being forearmed. Children can be guided to think things out for themselves, following that inner voice of intuition, inspiration and conscience, and then learning to taking the initiative instead of always following others.

Role models are sorely needed for moral courage and unfortunately, they seem to be in short supply amongst the rich and famous, but when examples are found, perhaps amongst friends and relatives and amongst children's own friends, these examples should be pointed out to children. Books, magazines and films can be watched for characters showing moral courage. The best source book I know is the Bible. Jesus must be the supreme example of moral courage, but such diverse characters as Nehemiah and Queen Ester are also good examples, as are Daniel and his compatriots – Shadrach, Meshach and Abed-Nego, famed for their refusal to worship the golden image, despite being cast into the burning fiery furnace, from which they emerged unscathed. How folks must have laughed at Noah for building a boat where no water was, but he was not deterred. Children love all these stories.

A boy, who knew the story of Daniel and admired his courage in the lion's den, left his infants' school and entered junior school. After being there only a few weeks, he saw something going on in the school that he felt was wrong, so he sought out the head teacher who put the matter right. That took real moral courage for a little boy in a new school.

Children should be taught the words "moral courage" and taught that it is even better to be morally than physically courageous. They should be brought up to understand that doing something just because everyone else is doing it, is not the right way to make decisions. The correct basis for decision making – to do something because it is right – is a lesson that needs to be thoroughly taught and shown by parental example.

Children can be told that when we do what is right, we are uniting with God and that there is a saying that "One with God is a majority."

Be alert, stand firm in the faith, be brave, be strong.

II Corinthians 16:13 GNB

Respect

In the minds of many, deference is dead. Traditional marks of respect like standing for the National Anthem are rarely seen, teachers are often called by their first names and children are not expected to stand when an adult enters the room. It is therefore no surprise that respect for older people and for authority is not so manifest in children today as it was formerly. Some TV shows today even encourage disrespect to adults. The Victorians, in an effort to instil respect for one's elders, maintained that "Children should be seen and not heard." Sometimes we stray too far from that motto and when parents are occupied, children are not made to wait to have their say. This is blatantly sowing the seeds of disrespect and disrespect can pave the way for physical violence.

Teaching respect for others should start in the early years, by teaching small children to wait their turn to speak instead of interrupting other people's conversations and children should be expected to maintain eye contact when speaking either to other children or to their elders. As soon as children are strong enough, instead of holding doors open for their children, parents should teach their children to hold doors open for their parents. Children need to be alerted to being thoughtful of others, which is what respect is all about. If this thoughtfulness is instilled in preteen years, it will be a great help during those years. Our rapidly changing world demands prompt action from adults to set guidelines for new situations, like, for example, mobile phone etiquette. Mobiles should be switched off at meal times and should never be answered in company without saying "Excuse me."

Like other virtues, respect must be learnt by example, a fact that was noted long ago by the philosopher John Locke, who wrote in 1693, "He that will have his son have respect for him and his orders, must himself have a great reverence for his son." *(Some Thoughts concerning Education)* Do I respect my child's individuality and recognise that I should be aiming to develop his individuality, and not to develop a clone of myself? If we wish children to have respect for adults, other people's feelings, for property and for living creatures, we must give them a good example to copy. Do I play fair and respect the law and do I respect those who enforce the law? Do I have respect for the point of view of others even when I don't agree with them? Do I credit my spouse with having a good idea, or do I usually think I've got a better one? Do I show respect for my own parents?

Even quite tiny babies know much of what is being said around them. Before a child speaks, he may recognise several hundred words and will understand others from the tone of voice being used. If you want your child to learn to be polite to you, then right from the start, give him an example of how to be gently spoken and polite.

Do you want your child to barge into your bedroom unannounced, or do you want him to knock? Then knock on his bedroom door. Respect your child's privacy, then he will learn to respect yours. Would you want your son or daughter to go through your private papers? Then never lay a finger on a teenager's diary.

I have a charming children's book that makes the point about respect in a delightful way. It is called *A Little House of Your Own*. After describing the various places where you can have a little house of your own (like under the table or in a big box) it finishes like this:

> When you are in your little house no one should bother you – if your mother has to tell you to get ready for dinner because it is dinnertime – then she should be very polite.
>
> She should walk softly and knock gently on the door of your little house and she should speak quietly and tell you, "Pretty soon it will be time to leave your little house and get ready for dinner."
>
> And if you should be walking near somebody's little house remember to be very polite
>
> walk softly
>
> speak gently.

Contacts with animals provide a good opportunity to exercise respect. Living creatures have rights to proper food, exercise and company; they also have rights that their bodies and their feelings be respected. One should never laugh at an animal that has fallen over or momentarily lost its dignity. To put it simply, it just isn't kind.

Then there's the matter of respect for property, an area where poor standards can be too readily accepted. "After all they're only children." Don't underestimate children's capabilities. My children were small when pre-school playgroups were just getting started and a group of mothers wanted to start a playgroup in our village and I was to be the supervisor. We had a village hall that could be used, but there were so many hurdles to be overcome in the way of safety requirements, permission for this and permission for that, that we began to doubt that we could get the playgroup up and running before some of the children were to start school.

We decided to begin with the eight children who were due to start school the following term and hold a mini playgroup in the playroom in our house, which was also our two daughters' bedroom. We had just had our staircase redecorated in a pastel shade and we didn't want little finger marks all over the walls. So, on the first morning I sat all the children down in the hall and explained to them about the decorating. I asked them to go upstairs holding on to the banisters and not to touch the walls. They all did as they were told and from thereafter a brief reminder sufficed and no child ever put so much as a finger on our walls.

Always treat a child's ideas with respect. If they are way off the mark, never ridicule them, but be gentle in your response. Never make a child feel foolish for having made a suggestion.

In lowliness of mind let each esteem other better than themselves.

Philippians 2:3

Responsibility

It is an observable fact that those with certain psychological problems are those who have not learnt to accept responsibility for their own actions and they blame others – usually their nearest and dearest – for their problems. This should alert us to the fact that teaching responsibility is a thing that should be taken very seriously and to beware of some of the currently "politically correct" ways of thinking which fudge this issue. In the long run it is positively harmful to children not to be made to face responsibility for their actions.

A new-born babe is completely dependent on others for his food, to be kept clean and warm and to be protected, but by the time a young person is 18 he should be competent to take entire responsibility for his own actions. Responsibility should therefore be introduced gradually, beginning at an early age. Toddlers can be taught to listen carefully to instructions and to obey them. Quite small children get great satisfaction from being asked to fetch and carry and should be allowed to help in this way. Learning perseverance when faced with a difficulty can also begin early.

During childhood years, parents should consciously nurture a child's confidence by only doing things for him that he is incapable of doing for himself. As soon as a child is able to do things like feeding himself, doing his own teeth, getting washed and dressed and tying shoelaces, let him get on with it. It is easier for you, and he gets a sense of achievement in taking responsibility for himself. Early potty training, thought not currently fashionable, gives a toddler a great sense of achievement. Parents should never hold back their child's progress; true mother-love does not want to keep a child dependent on herself, – that is smother love, not mother love.

If a child is given responsibility he will respond well to the trust that is placed in him. Children who are given tasks to do that are within their abilities or that present a modest challenge, should be left to get on with the job without the parent constantly hovering over them – an action that says, "I'm worried in case you make a mess of this," and which is likely to become a self-fulfilling prophecy. Children will be careful if you trust them and don't be anxious. Older siblings enjoy helping with their younger brothers and sisters.

Decision-making needs to be introduced thoughtfully into a child's experience. If pushed upon a child too early, the child will become burdened, for making decisions demands a certain degree of knowledge. I've always thought it a good idea for children, as early as possible, to have some say in the choice of clothes they will wear – after all they are the ones who will be wearing them. If the mother makes a selection of two or three garments, any of which would be suitable, then lets the child have the final choice, the child is pleased and begins to feel some control over his destiny.

Children are helped by taking responsibility for certain jobs around the house – table laying and clearing being the first jobs most children do. They respond to being allowed to wash up much better than being expected to dry – after all, water is a lot more fun, isn't it?

During school holidays, I expected our children to help with extra chores in the house. It freed me and was good for them. Each one had a regular job to do at meal times, and each day in the holidays we had a job list, which I put up in the kitchen before I went to bed. It would have three things that needed doing (we had three children) and the first one down got the pick of the jobs which varied from dusting or polishing somewhere to peeling potatoes or emptying the waste bins. Competition to get the choice of jobs had the additional bonus of prizing them out of bed in the morning.

When the family grew older, I felt it was time for them to do their own ironing, and I thought that boys too, should learn to iron. But I had reckoned without economic forces, for by this time our son was at work and promptly offered to pay his sisters who were still at school to do his ironing for him! I conceded defeat on that one.

Taking responsibility for your own actions is something that can be learned at a tender age; if you make a mess, you clear it up (if possible) and you apologise to the person who was at the receiving end of your mistake.

Be ready to recognise the stages in your child's development as he matures and respect and nurture his independence instead of fearing it, then your child will, in later years, have much to thank you for.

That our sons may be as plants grown up, in their youth; that our daughters may be as corner stones, polished after the similitude of a palace.   Psalms 144:12

Gentleness

Violence is frequently linked with a desire to have power over another sentient being, either human or animal and it is a fact that most serial killers started on the pathway to murder by abusing animals when they were children. This is why some police forces now work in conjunction with the RSPCA in an effort to halt the spread of abuse from animals to humans.

The dictionary has some interesting comments in connection with the word gentle. Its opposites are listed as rough, harsh, stern, wild, turbulent, refractory, violent, loud, disturbing. We certainly don't want to bring children up with any of those qualities, so learning gentleness is an invaluable antidote to such undesirable characteristics. Anger also is the antithesis of gentleness and needs subduing, or it will provide the roots from which physical violence may grow. An atmosphere of calm and quiet on the part of parents is conducive to developing gentleness in children.

A poem by David Bates, begins:

Speak gently, it is better far
To rule by love than fear;
Speak gently, let no harsh word mar
The good we may do here.

My dictionary also says that gentle describes the natural disposition. Drawing out a child's natural gentleness can begin very early by showing babies and toddlers how to treat their soft toys and any pets with gentleness. Show them how to stroke a dog or cat the right way of the fur and how not to try to force a little animal to do things it doesn't want to do. They need to learn to treat younger siblings with sensitivity for their feelings. It really goes without saying, that if you want little boys to be gentle – *don't let them have toy guns.*

Because of their superior physical strength, gentleness has historically been especially esteemed in men. That is in no way diminished today and a boy who eschews a "macho" image and matures into a real gentleman is one who will command both respect and affection.

Gentleness helps to develop a child's immunity to antisocial behaviour and is closely linked with the next quality to be considered.

Thy gentleness hath made me great.   Psalms 18:35

Kindness

George Eliot wrote the following passage, which she called The Essence of Friendship. "Oh, the comfort, the inexpressible comfort of feeling safe with a person; having neither to weigh thoughts nor measure words, but to pour them all out, just as they are, chaff and grain together, knowing that a faithful hand will take and sift them, keep what is worth keeping, and then, with the breath of kindness, blow the rest away."

That breath of kindness is much needed in the world and showing a child how to be kind to others is one of the simplest lessons you will ever teach. Many of the things for which a child needs to be corrected can be covered by the simple reminder: "Don't do that, its not kind" which every child will find perfectly easy to understand.

Children should be taught to appreciate kindness when it is shown to them – when they are given a present or when another child shares a toy, "That was kind". When such instances are pointed out, the child will come to understand the benefits of kindness and will have more motivation to be kind himself. His own acts of kindness should be appreciated too and rewarded. To keep a "Kindness Book" where deeds of kindness are recorded is an excellent project for a playgroup, school class or for a family.

Kindness means including, not excluding, others, it means waiting one's turn, it involves being sensitive to the needs of others and meeting those needs whenever possible; it is thoughtfulness, compassion, patience and unselfishness rolled into one; it is love in action. Kindness directly benefits the one who is the recipient of the kindness, but blesses the benefactor even more, especially when self-sacrifice is called for.

All living creatures – not just humans – should have kindness shown to them. This puts a question mark over an activity beloved of many small boys, namely fishing. Parents should ponder if they will allow it and if so, with what restraints.

Frey Ellis, who was at one-time Consultant Haematologist for the Kingston and Richmond area of Surrey and President of the Vegan Society from 1964 until his passing in 1978, had some telling observations about kindness. His comments add a medical dimension to the effect of being kind. Here are some extracts from one of his addresses:

> Kindness is an actual power which exists in us but does not appear to be part of our material body. It is an external and invisible power, like electricity, which we can and do use in our everyday life. We recognise this power which we call kindness by its inner effects upon our brain and mind. When used properly it produces in the body and mind, the feeling of peace, joy and enthusiasm, as well as enabling us to obtain harmony with all our external affairs, including our relationship with other people. The correct use of kindness is essential for continuous happiness.

Abuse of any kind is an apparent lack of kindness and Frey Ellis went on to say,

> Our bodies and minds are made up so that we may experience love, joy and peace. If then we allow our minds and bodies to practice the reverse, that is cruelty, we are using them wrongly and inevitably some or all of our tissues will depart from normal activity and hence a disease process is initiated. We all know that before acting in an unkind manner, it is necessary to harden our hearts. The physiology of this process has, to my knowledge, never been investigated.

> Whatever may be the changes brought about in the chemical structure of our body tissues by this process it is obviously detrimental to our health. If we deliberately allow this process to continue daily, monthly and yearly, we will eventually produce such changes in our body that it will no longer be able to fulfil its normal functions. . . . I believe that many of the chronic and degenerative diseases that beset us today are caused by this process and that we will not be free of them until we learn to act always with compassion.

Never forget to show kindness and to share what you have with others.
. . .   Hebrews 13:16, NEB

Restraint

The quality of restraint is closely allied to moderation and neither is in vogue at the moment. Restraint is learning to hold back an unkind or personal remark (children need careful training in understanding not to make personal remarks), learning not to take the biggest cake that's offered, and not giving way to frustration. If we don't learn restraint, we're like someone driving a car at high speed, but with no brakes and in both cases, the consequences can be disastrous.

A young boy was once visiting his grandparents who kindly invited a neighbour's boy of the same age to play with the grandson. The two boys were playing cricket together on the lawn. The problem was that there were two lawns in the garden and the grandparents wanted the boys to use the smaller lawn that was further from the house (and its windows). After a couple of warnings about playing on the lower lawn, which were ignored, the grandmother told the grandson off quite sharply. Grandson promptly flung his cricket bat down on the grass. "Joshua, come here!" said grandma and when Joshua came, he was roundly told off for venting his annoyance in that way. I must confess, I'd have been tempted to let it go, but I saw how right the grandmother had been

Restraint goes out of the window when well-meaning, affluent parents and grandparents load up children with too many presents. They don't stop to think what effect their unrestrained giving is having on the mentality of the recipients. Many children nowadays are so inundated with material possessions that

(1)   They cannot appreciate them properly
(2)   It is too much for them to keep tidy and care for
(3)   Greed and selfishness are being encouraged, and
(4)   Having too many possessions takes away the joy in having
        something new.

This is not meant to be an argument against the giving of expensive presents, merely to question the wisdom of accumulating too many at once. Some parents find the answer lies in having regular clear-outs of toys for charity, which has the added advantage of helping children to think of others.

Britain boasts the highest consumption of sweets per head of any country and a quick look around a supermarket shows how sweets are used to pacify fretful children whose mothers are afraid they will raise a rumpus if they don't get what they want. Right from this early stage in their young lives, children are being allowed to indulge themselves with no sense of moderation whatsoever. Is it any wonder that in later years their lack of restraint develops into habits that have more serious consequences?

All too often, children rub each other up. "He upset me" "She annoyed me" and other grumbles arise from thoughtless behaviour on the part of another child. But wait – you don't have to react, you can show restraint in your response. I sometimes explain it in this way to a child, "It is like having a ball thrown at you; you can either catch it, or you can let it drop to the ground." Don't 'catch' the unkind remark and send one back – just let it 'fall to the ground.' Don't pick it up. Someone may try to annoy you, but it's up to you whether or not you let them do that to you." There is nothing to stop you from restraining your feelings when you have a genuine desire to do so.

Another way of exercising restraint is to resist the temptation to gossip. If you have information that would hurt or upset someone else, learn to keep it to yourself – forget it if you can. This becomes easier with practice and eventually becomes the natural thing to do. Beware, however, of expecting too much in the way of restraint over the keeping of secrets. This is too demanding for small children and it is better not to expect this of them. I once talked with a class of six-year olds about keeping secrets. One little boy was very eager to share his experience. "I know what a secret is," he said, "It's something you don't tell other people. My Daddy brought some biscuits back from work and Mummy said I shouldn't tell anyone. That's a secret, isn't it?"

He that keepeth his mouth keepeth his life.   Proverbs 13:3

Gratitude

Gratitude is being aware of goodness that comes into our life and saying "Thank you" for it. I have observed that the expression of gratitude is an unseen line of demarcation between the well-rounded, poised individual and the insecure and maladjusted individual. The habit of gratitude paves the way for other social graces, a sentiment, which is well expressed in a verse from a hymn:

A grateful heart a garden
  Where there is always room
For every lovely, Godlike grace
  To come to perfect bloom.

A lovely story that emerged at the time of the passing of Diana, Princess of Wales, was of Diana's promptness in saying "Thank you." As a child her father had taught her "If you don't say 'Thank you' within 48 hours, then it's not worth saying." Say as many "Thank you's" as you can and insist that children write Christmas "Thank you" letters before New Year arrives.

Gratitude is a wonderful healer. It helps to heal sorrow and complaints for you cannot feel full of gratitude and be miserable at the same time – it is an impossibility. If a child is being grumpy, get him to make either a verbal or written gratitude list. A list can be started with the obvious, straightforward things, your loved ones, prized possessions, happy memories etc, but then you have to dig deeper, to the so-called "intangibles" which can be the most precious of all because they can't be taken away. You can be grateful for a kindness shown to you, grateful for opportunities to do good and grateful for character improvements – the list really is endless.

The habit of being grateful means that there is no room for greed and less room for worry, which has been called ingratitude in advance. Gratitude is a quality that is well worth cultivating and preferable to grumbles any day. Try it for yourself and encourage your children in the gratitude habit. Get them to think of something for which they can be grateful every night when they are tucked up in bed and tell them the things that they have done that day for which you are grateful. Help children to resist the temptation to grumble. If parents are tempted to grumble at each other —DON'T. Hold your tongue and instead think of something you can be grateful for in each other – it makes for much more pleasant days.

One mother who was determined that her little boy would grow up to be appreciative of what others did for him, regularly asked him, "Who washes your clothes?" "Who gets your meals ready?" etc. One morning he said, "Thank you for dressing me Mummy" and another day (with no prompting) "Thank you for my dinner." This child's good manners now make him a joy to be with. Teaching a child to appreciate others is also a wonderful way to prevent shyness. If you are so busy concentrating on and appreciating what others are doing, then you are no longer focussing on yourself and your (perceived) shortcomings.

Rejoice evermore   I Thessalonians 5:16

Generosity

Generosity is being the one to initiate doing good with no thought of whether the recipient will be able to reciprocate. Generosity is giving freely. Giving what? Giving pleasure, joy and happiness is what it is all about; the chocolates, the flowers, the toys, or whatever, are the means of achieving this end. Generous people are always happy, so give freely and unstintingly. Mother Teresa once said, "It is not how much we give but how much love we put into the giving."

One year I was doing my annual house to house collecting for charity – I'd delivered the little envelopes and now it was time to collect them. I went to one house and rang the bell. After a while a little girl appeared, I'd say she was too young to go to school. "Is your mummy there?" I asked. "She's asleep," was the reply, "What have you come for?" I explained that I was collecting money to help animals. Immediately the little girl said, "I'll give you some money. I'll get my money box".

"You didn't take her money, did you?" asked a friend when I told the story. I did take her money, for I know that being generous is satisfying and I didn't want to deprive the child of that satisfaction. I wanted her to feel that joy of giving.

Children should be encouraged to give, both of their possessions and of themselves and to do it cheerfully and not grudgingly.

One of my enduring memories is from my early twenties when I was visiting the United States. A crowd of young people took me to swim in Lake Huron, but I didn't have a swimsuit with me. The girl I was staying with lent me her brand new swimsuit, whilst she wore her old one. Her generosity made such an impression on me, because I knew how much she must have wanted to wear the new one herself. Hopefully we can learn generosity from others and I am grateful to the friends who have taught me never to return a container empty, always to print off an extra set of photos for sharing, to be generous in giving time to others and to give presents not just when you are visiting someone, but to those who are visiting you.

But beware the subtle trap that lies in wait for good parents – that of being so concerned about doing things for your children that they end up always expecting to be on the receiving end of the handouts. Insist that your children think of things to do for you as well as for other people. **Don't be such unselfish parents that you raise selfish children.**

God loveth a cheerful giver.   II Corinthians 9:7

Honesty

Sir Walter Scott wrote,

O what a tangled web we weave,
When first we practice to deceive

Any child who has told a lie, been questioned, and told another lie to cover up for the first, experiences the truth of that saying. Lying is the one thing that all known criminals have in common so parents shouldn't wish to set an example to their children of doing something that criminals do.

If you want your child to tell the truth, then always, ALWAYS tell him the truth, no matter what it costs. Too many parents are not completely honest with their children and tell "white" lies when it is inconvenient to tell the truth. Because of their position they may get away with this when children are small, but it is a terrible habit to get into and when the children grow older they will suss it out and their respect for their parents is, justifiably, eroded, to say nothing of their respect for honesty. Saying, "I'm too busy to go now" may really mean, "Its not convenient" or "I can't be bothered". "No, its not got mushrooms in it" may equal "I chopped them up small in the hope that you won't notice them". Another form of dishonesty is sneaking out of the room in case a toddler sees you going and starts to wail.

Its dishonest to take a young child to see a film that is classified for older children, even if big brother is old enough.

It may seem surprising, but practically all parents have the habit of lying to their children on a regular and knowing basis. They do it in the mistaken belief that they are giving the child innocent enjoyment and I refer to misleading children into believing that Santa Claus either gives or delivers their Christmas presents. When children eventually find out the truth, some of them feel badly hurt that their parents have deceived them in this way and it can take quite a time before they feel they can trust their parents again. We never deceived our children; we hung up stockings on Christmas Eve just like everyone else and the fun was in no way diminished because our children knew who Santa was, in fact they all felt "one up" on other kids who didn't know what they knew.

Children should be made to understand that the most severe punishment for lying is not one that is imposed upon them by parents or teachers, but the one that arises from their own action – that a liar may not be believed when he tells the truth, a fact that children find very frustrating.

If children do lie, it is usually because they are afraid of getting into trouble if they admit to doing wrong, therefore the best way to prevent children from lying is to maintain an atmosphere of love and trust, which your own transparent honesty will encourage. A child who knows his parents trust him is less likely to tell a lie but if your child does lie, he will need gentle help in getting out of the hole he's got into. He will need support in admitting what he has done and apologising to the one he lied to.

In addition to being truthful, honesty means respecting other people's privacy and not looking into their cupboards, drawers, bags etc. It means not borrowing without permission. It's well worth the effort, for scrupulous honesty gives a feeling of wellbeing.

Provide things honest in the sight of all men.   Romans 12:17

Patience

After love, patience is arguably the most important quality needed by those dealing with the education of children, be they parents or teachers, and it is closely allied to self-control. Can we expect children to learn self-control if we fly off the handle when provoked instead of quietly persisting with what is required? Lack of patience is always a factor in the horror stories we hear about parents or carers ill-treating children.

Parents should recognise that children each have their own pace of learning and that they need encouragement not to give up when something is hard for them. Some parents loose patience when their child doesn't 'come top' in everything he does, which is very disheartening for a child and very unfair on him too. Adults need to exercise patience with impatient children and encourage and help them to complete jobs that need doing; they can firmly insist on not permitting a child to give up.

Patience isn't dull or boring, it isn't just doing nothing while you wait for something to happen; it is an active quality. It is constancy in labour or application, it is quietness and self-possession under provocation; it is calmness in operation.

Two factors today work against the application of patience, these are the increased speed of society and modern educational methods. As a society, we expect things to happen instantly and whilst no one could deny the many benefits that this brings, it frequently obviates the need for patience. Modern education focuses on freeing each child to progress according to his own ability, whereas old-fashioned ways were structured to greater uniformity. For example, when I was teaching infants to write I took this as a class lesson, but inevitably some children took longer than others to form the letters. I figured that for the quicker ones, to learn to wait for the others was as important in its own way, as learning to write, so I was teaching two lessons in one.

There is also a trend nowadays to change the basic format of school sports days. Instead of having traditional races, all the children are constantly engaged in different group activities. This not only does away with the excitement of competing in front of an audience but also with the need to wait for your turn to race. "They get fed up with waiting" was one justification I heard from a teacher, quite overlooking the value of learning patience.

Patience is what enables a child to persist in perfecting a new skill; patience is what is needed when he gets something wrong and has to correct it. Children need to wait patiently for their turn to speak, and as a general rule, they should wait at the table, when they have finished eating, until others have finished too.

Have you ever considered that patience can make you safe? If not, then think for a moment about young motor bikers. These young men usually have great skill in handing their machines, which have an aura of freedom, power and independence. To many riders the temptation to ignore the rules of the road as well as the markings thereon is strong. They see the opportunity to take advantage of their slim, powerful vehicles to weave in and out of traffic jams and to overtake when wisdom decrees caution. They are impatient to get by and speed ahead. The idea of patience would probably seem dull in the extreme, yet it could save many a fatal accident.

Patience (like all other necessary good qualities) is not a personal possession that can either wear thin or run out. It is the gift of God to all His children and it is given freely so if yours appears to be hidden, its like buried treasure, worth digging for. One thing is certain, that if you hold the mistaken but commonly accepted belief that you are not a patient person, then the harder you are making it for yourself to be patient. If, on the other hand, you believe that patience must be there, waiting to be used, then you have already broken down the biggest barrier. Mentally refute the suggestion that you lack anything you need and start digging for your hidden treasure! Patience is there for you in abundance waiting to be used.

God giveth not the Spirit by measure. . . .   John 3:34

Forgiveness

A little girl came bursting out of school in a hurry to tell her mother what had happened that day. Another child had deliberately got her into trouble and she hadn't done what she was accused of doing! The hurt feelings had grown during the day and she was just longing for the sympathy she knew she deserved. How unfair it all was!

Her mother's response shook her rigid. "Forgive her" was all she said. That simple act is all that is needed to deflate hurt pride. Teaching forgiveness is one of the most neglected aspects of moral training, for parents are commonly so involved in getting to the bottom of trouble between children and so anxious that their children learn to stand up for themselves that forgiveness is seldom taught.

On the occasions when one has done something one shouldn't have done, how wonderful it is when a friend makes nothing of it! "That's all right" they say, "think no more of it." What a relief! Practice forgiveness and it will benefit you even more than the one you forgive. Teach children that if you really forgive, you don't think about what was done any more, and you just act towards your friend as though what they did never happened at all. Forgive your children when a wrong is sorted out; just draw a line under the incident.

In a marriage, it can be tempting to "score points" yet how futile this is. What's the point when your aim should be to make your marriage a success and have a happy home? If you believe your spouse has wronged you, if you are feeling hurt, neglected or upset – NEVER settle for the night without making it up, for resentment is like a cumulative poison, it builds up. If there has been trouble with a child, clear the air with them before they go to sleep.

Many people have written and said helpful things about forgiveness. Mary Livermore, a nineteenth-century American prison reformer wrote,

Jesus, what precept is like thine:
Forgive, as ye would be forgiven;
If heeded, O what power divine
Would then transform our earth to heaven.

Debbie Morris, whose real life experience was made into a motion picture, has much to say about forgiveness in her book, *Forgiving the Dead Men Walking*. In 1980, Debbie and her boyfriend were parked in their car late at night, when they were attacked. During the next 30 hours the boyfriend was tortured, while Debbie endured a frightening night of brutality and rape. She finally managed to escape from her captors but her boyfriend died.

For years Debbie suffered from anxiety and depression and eventually succumbed to alcoholism. Despite that struggle she bravely assisted in the trial of her abductor and comforted other victims and their parents. She finally came to the realisation that to rebuild her life she must forgive her abductors. She writes, "Even before Robert Wilkie was executed . . . I knew I had to forgive him – not for his sake, but for mine. Until I did, there was no escaping the hold evil had on my life."

Gordon Wilson, whose daughter Marie died in his arms following the IRA bombing in Enniskillen in 1987, said he bore no malice and forgave the bombers. Nelson Mandela's spirit of forgiveness had national impact when South Africa made the transition to black rule.

A couple whose son-in-law physically abused their daughter until she could take no more and the marriage ended, told me, "We have forgiven him for the sake of our little granddaughter who still loves her Daddy. He visits us and we give him a present at Christmas." When one thinks of people having enough love in their hearts to forgive those who murdered and abused their loved ones, it shouldn't seem so hard to forgive less heinous actions.

Anna Campbell Stark wrote these words:

Teach me to forgive
Dear Father in heaven.
Then help me to forget
That I have forgiven.

That always seems to me to be the completion of it all – let it all go – forget it. If someone says, "I'll forgive, but I'll never forget," they haven't really forgiven. Forgiveness includes forgetting – letting go. Why should it seem hard to say, "I'm sorry" and open the door to forgiveness?

It is always sad to hear of families where one member of the family has not been in touch with others over a period of years, following an old misunderstanding or hurt. How much simpler if there had been forgiveness as Joseph (who had the Amazing Technicolour Dreamcoat) forgave the brothers who had tried to kill him.

Never miss an opportunity to teach your child to forgive.

Then came Peter to him, and said, "Lord, how oft shall my brother sin against me, and I forgive him? till seven times?" Jesus saith unto him, "I say not unto thee, Until seven times: but, Until seventy times seven."
Matthew 18:21,22

Commitment

Adults who enjoy a commitment to a worthwhile activity, an activity that demands something of them and from which they reap great satisfaction, can appreciate the value to children of being involved with activities that do the same for them. Such activities may be as diverse as playing football or basketball, going swimming or diving, reading books, collecting things, playing an instrument or doing some form of voluntary work. Interest may be sparked off by a parent's own interest, by a book, by the Internet, by a TV programme or by what one's friends are doing. Whatever the activity is, to be focussed on something that gives direction to your life and increases your knowledge and experience helps children to feel good about themselves.

Children may be committed to one thing at one time and another thing at another time, and this is good, for it gives them a wider sphere of interest and opportunities for social contacts. Having a particular interest provides a topic of conversation and encourages an introverted or shy child to think of other things and other people instead of being preoccupied with himself. Increased self-confidence is a by-product of commitment.

I also link commitment with enthusiasm for one who is really committed to a particular activity inevitably is enthusiastic about it, and I love this definition of enthusiasm: Inspired by God. Enthusiasm is a mixture of vitality and cheerfulness. The enthusiastic are lively and get things done. They smile a lot and their eyes are alight with interest as they listen to what others are saying. They don't bemoan their difficulties, but set about overcoming them. They are the most active people around and are never bored, so a quality like commitment that leads to enthusiasm should never be underrated.

Sadly, all too often, commitment is undervalued for it is erroneously perceived as a limitation, instead of being viewed as a springboard for satisfaction and achievement. Lack of commitment is a reason why many marriages fail, why some organisations that depend upon voluntary labour struggle to survive and it is why so many children and teens are bored.

Children who are committed to a particular activity and are enthusiastic about it are growing up with an in-built immunity against the problem of depression in future years. Procrastination, apathy, indifference and lethargy characterise those who suffer from depression and commitment and enthusiasm are an antidote for them all.

And whatsoever ye do, do it heartily. . . .   Colossians 3:23

I have included what I feel to be the most important of the many moral and spiritual qualities. There will no doubt be other qualities that you feel are important to teach and which you will find ways to impart to your children. I would recommend the *Book of Virtues, a Treasury of Great Moral Stories* as a wonderful resource for teaching the value of good qualities. The book reinforces some of the qualities discussed here and introduces others. Whilst good qualities are important in themselves, their great significance is that they are our link with the divine Mind – the essence of our relationship with God. By exercising good qualities we are yielding our mentality to that great spiritual power within, and this divine source should be acknowledged.

Concerning spiritual gifts, brethren, I would not have you ignorant.
I Corinthians 12:1

I first saw this anonymous poem when my husband brought it back from a business trip to San Francisco – it was printed on a piece of white felt and it hung in our house during all the years when our children were growing up and we constantly referred to it. I have since seen it in other places, but it bears repeating.

CHILDREN LEARN WHAT THEY LIVE

If a child lives with criticism
He learns to condemn.

If a child lives with hostility
He learns to fight.

If a child lives with ridicule
He learns to be shy.

If a child lives with jealousy
He learns to feel guilty.

If a child lives with tolerance
He learns to be patient.

If a child lives with encouragement
He learns confidence.

If a child lives with praise
He learns to appreciate.

If a child lives with fairness
He learns justice.

If a child lives with security
He learns to have faith.

If a child lives with approval
He learns to like himself.

If a child lives with acceptance and friendship
He learns to find love in the world.

V. The Ten Rules of Happiness

What part of "Thou shalt not" didn't you understand? – God
(One of a series of billboards seen in the United States)

One half of the world cannot understand the pleasures of the other
Jane Austen (Emma)

Mankind has always sought out the means to be happy and the ways in which they obtain happiness are infinitely diverse. Try telling those who are hooked on drugs or sex that the greatest satisfaction is in giving and they'd look at you blankly, thinking you naïve, ignorant or just plain foolish. What brings enduring joy and satisfaction must be one of the most important questions to answer, and to answer rightly.

We need guidelines to follow if we are to grow into a higher sense of what constitutes real happiness, and surely none have proved their worth more adequately than the laws that were first put to the test over three thousand years ago when a mass migration was under way in the Middle East. Hebrew slaves were fleeing from the land of Egypt where they had been in bondage for generations. Their thankfulness for being freed from slavery soon turned to grumbles about the difficulties of their journey. They became quarrelsome and the leader of the group was worn out with trying to solve all their problems. Then it became clear to him that the people needed instruction on how to think and how to behave towards one another, in short they needed moral laws.

The leader was Moses, the migrants were the children of Israel and the Ten Commandments were the moral laws. Knowledge of these laws improved the lot of the Hebrews and gave them a basis for solving their problems. The commandments, however are more than *moral* laws; they have a *spiritual* foundation which is why obeying them brings true happiness and freedom. Alfred the Great himself translated the Ten Commandments into English and made them the basis of laws in Britain, from whence they in turn influenced the laws in the United States and of all countries that once formed the British Empire.

The historic journey taken by the Children of Israel out of the land of bondage into the promised land can serve as a modern day parable, for the ten commandments lead all who follow them out of the bondage of self-centred and materialistic thinking into the freedom and wellbeing that comes from obedience to the right. In a conversation I had recently with a Chinese student who was searching for answers to life's deeper questions, I briefly stated my formula for happiness and satisfaction – to live in accord with what is *right*.

"What a wonderful way to live," she said.

"It's the only way to live," I replied, for are we *really* living, when we are asleep to higher joys?

The commandments restrain anti-social behaviour by serving as stop signs to warn of the dangers of deviating from the "straight and narrow way" of truth and goodness.

The first two commandments get right to the nitty-gritty of the way men need to think in order to lead more spiritual lives; the first five speak of our relationship with God and the latter six speak of relations between men. No, I've not miscounted, for number five can be applied in two different ways.

1. Thou shalt have no other gods before me

The First Commandment is the Big One! It sets the standard of thinking that embraces all the others. Before we consider how to obey it, we have to ponder what this "me" indicates. I find it helps to sort it out like this:

When people anywhere speak of God, or Allah, or Jehovah or whatever, they are speaking of a Creator – a First Cause. I therefore define this Creator as:

That which is self-existent; that which did not have to be created.

God is Truth. God must be Truth, for isn't this a way of expressing self-existence – that which doesn't have to be created – that which just **is**? Whatever is true in the big scheme of things could not have been created – it just *is*. Children should be taught that God is Truth, for to have no other God than Truth highlights the importance of expressing honesty, truthfulness, reliability, steadfastness and integrity – qualities which emanate from Truth.

God is Spirit says the New English Bible (John 4:24). This definition of God helps children understand how something can be present, yet invisible to the mortal senses. Spirit can be likened to the wind, for neither is visible to the eyes, but the presence of both can be clearly discerned. Wind causes trees and shrubs to move, it whips up waves on the sea and we can feel its cooling effect. Similarly Spirit is the unseen mental force that acts for good upon people's thinking, children and adults alike. It motivates us to act in ethical and thoughtful ways and its guiding presence in the mind can be clearly felt.

Ask anyone who is a dedicated charity worker why they do the charity work and they will tell you it's because they want to help, they might even say they feel *impelled* to do it. Ask any honest man why he does not steal and he will tell you he wouldn't want to do such a thing; maybe he'll even tell you he *couldn't* do it. Most people feel that force for good in their consciousness – yet don't always associate it with Deity.

God is the divine Mind for what is it that thinks but a Mind? The prophet Jeremiah said, referring to God, "I know the thoughts that I think towards you" (29:11) and much has already been said about God as the divine Mind, the source of all good thoughts. Children should be taught that the vital and essential message of the first commandment is to listen to and obey good thoughts. Those who are brought up to identify God as the source of inner guidance and taught to obey good impulses are having their lives set on a course that will give them courage and security. They will grow up to understand that God is a living reality whom they can learn to trust.

"God is Love" (I John 4:8). If we claim that we are worshipping God yet are devoid of love to others, then our life is a sham. To express the various components of love – kindness, patience, gentleness and the like – is the surest way to feel your unity with divine Love and using these and other qualities (as discussed in the last chapter) is a way of obeying this first commandment.

God is Father and Mother. For many centuries we have thought of God as our Father, but it is comparatively recently that the idea of God as our Mother has become more accepted, and this is a wonderful concept for children to be taught, for Mother-love generates the idea of comfort and tenderness and to ponder God as a spiritual Mother sets the purest standard for human parenthood. When individuals are motivated by pure love, they feel a unity with their Creator. There is a couplet that expresses this sentiment beautifully. I do not know who wrote it, but it goes like this:

I am the one that God shines through;
He and I are one, not two.

Letting God's love shine through you is the surest way to feel your unity with Spirit. It is only by obeying the first commandment that individuals can discover the inner spiritual core of their being and can awaken to their relationship with their Maker.

God is the spiritual origin of all that is good. This first commandment is a call to acknowledge this fact; it is telling us to focus on those things which are physically intangible yet are the essential spiritual factors in all aspects of life. Commerce cannot function without honesty, marriage cannot succeed without unselfishness, scientific advances are not made without thoroughness and stock markets slump when confidence is eroded. Honesty, unselfishness, thoroughness and confidence are not physically tangible, but they are the vital components without which human lives and human activity cannot function satisfactorily. Spirit is their origin, therefore Spirit needs to be our God and the commandment highlights the need to train the thoughts of future generations to penetrate beyond the realm of matter into the realm of more enlightened, spiritual consciousness.

Obedience to this commandment is the underlying theme of Mary Baker Eddy's work *Science and Health with Key to the Scriptures* which I commend to all seeking to appreciate the commandment's wide implications.

> Thou shalt love the Lord thy God with all thy heart, and with all thy soul, and with all thy mind.   Matthew 22:37

2. Thou shalt not make unto thee any graven image, or any likeness of any thing that is in the heaven above, or that is in the earth beneath, or that is in the water under the earth. Thou shalt not bow down thyself to them nor serve them

In broad terms, I see this commandment as alerting us to those things which would cause one to deviate from obeying the First Commandment. There are various mental influences which would counter the beneficial influence of the one Mind in one's consciousness. For example, the panic that passes through a crowd when something causes alarm can be hard to resist. Go to a meeting when feelings run high and it is easy to be swayed by a speaker who carries the crowd with them. For children, peer pressure is usually the biggest hurdle to overcome in this regard. Other mental influences are more subtle or obscure and show themselves in unreasoning anxiety or in a build up of mental pressure. It is helpful to children to be alerted to these spurious influences.

Let's consider *graven image*s. The commandment does not refer merely to the images that were graven in wood or stone and worshipped by primitive peoples. It can refer to images which can easily impress themselves on the minds of children and adults today and which can mislead the young into accepting materialistic values. What images are you allowing to be engraved into your children's minds? Do you monitor what your children see on television, films, computer games and what pop music they hear? Do you help them to be discriminating and sensitive and not to be carried away by degrading images?

What image do you have of children? As we have seen, the images that adults have of a child help to shape the child's own image of himself.

Refusing to have outward appearances engraved in your mind was the secret of Father Flanagan's success, and is a secret we can all share.

Then there is the question of *likenesses of things*. Here the topic of forgeries is a helpful analogy. A forgery, whether it's of a work of art or a bank note, aims to be like the original and aims to fool people into believing it's the genuine thing. If, for example, we allow children to accept hatred, resentment or prejudice when thinking of others we are allowing them to be fooled by the outward appearance when we should be teaching them to see beyond those appearances. Are we allowing children to accept either inferiority or superiority in regard to themselves? Any of these will be detrimental to their moral and spiritual progress.

When one strives to keep mentally close to the divine Mind by cultivating thoughts that are good and pure, impulses that would pull one down are progressively silenced, just as an aeroplane resists the pull of gravity and flies above the clouds. To guide children into the mental state that habitually listens to and obeys the one Mind – and no other – is the sum total of how to raise good children.

And what I say unto you I say unto all, Watch.   Mark 13:37

The following two commandments are often regarded as outdated, but I don't believe they are.

3. Thou shalt not take the name of the Lord thy God in vain

If this commandment appears to be irrelevant in today's world then pause to consider our blasphemy laws. These were originally enacted because those who "took the Lord's name in vain" and used words like "God" and "Jesus" in an irreverent manner were likely to suffer violence from outraged Christians **therefore for their own protection** such utterances were forbidden by law. It is commonly overlooked that blasphemy laws were written for the protection of the blasphemer, yet only those who offended against *Christian* beliefs were entitled to that protection.

As Britain became more multicultural, it would have been a natural adjustment to extend the blasphemy laws to include non-Christian religions, but this was never done. (Such legislation would have brought a different approach to the Salmon Rushdie case).

Schools now make a strong point of teaching understanding of and respect for non-Christian religions, which is a praiseworthy thing, but are children being taught the same respect for the Christian religion? The Founder of Christianity had a huge influence for good in this world and great respect is due to him. Children must be taught not to use his name in an irreverent manner. Likewise to use the name "God" as a swear word indicates an ignorance of God and children should neither be allowed to do this in their home, nor out of it. If I hear any child using God's name irreverently, I say, "God is my Friend, so please don't say His name like that." Some parents teach their children a suitable alternative phrase like, "Oh my goodness," which is a helpful idea.

When God's name is taken in vain the blasphemer is usually in an agitated state and not in full command of himself, which is in line with what the word "vain" means "destitute of force or energy, effecting no purpose, fruitless, ineffectual." If children are to be taught to control their speech, then having a right example is of paramount importance. Our environment would be more pleasant if this so-called "outdated" commandment were obeyed and offensive language was not fed into the minds of impressionable children.

> Not that which goes into the mouth defileth a man; but that which cometh out of the mouth, this defileth a man.
>
>   Matthew 15:11

4. Remember the sabbath day to keep it holy

The Sabbath is literally a season or day of rest and the word sabbatical is derived from it. The ancient Hebrews were the first to institute a day of rest. The satisfaction we feel when a job is completed should be savoured – "kept holy". Regardless of whether one uses the Sabbath for church going or as a family day – or both – it is pleasant to have one day of the week that is different from the others, for a pause in the busy routine is refreshing. It is very dull to have every day like every other.

But there is a very different application of this commandment and a deeper meaning of how to keep our Sabbath days holy. This fourth commandment has its roots in an earlier part of the Bible, namely, the first chapter of Genesis. Here we read an inspired account of creation (so different from the more popular Adam and Eve story) which speaks of creation as taking place on six days, and then states that when creation was complete "God saw everything that he had made, and, behold, it was very good." (Genesis 1:31) Later, the Bible tells us that God rested on the seventh day.

To see that everything is "very good" as God sees it is to behold that ever-present inner goodness instead of focussing on those outward appearances.

This isn't easy! It calls for great patience, prayer and persistence. It may be an almighty struggle involving great mental discipline and the six "days" it takes are not measured by calendars, but can be likened to the steps of mental progress needed to clear out criticism, condemnation, or other ungodlike qualities that cloud our inner vision. We need to continue to work and pray for our "six days" then we will finally reach a "day" of rest when we feel at peace and an assurance that our prayers are answered. This was well illustrated by the mental work and prayer undertaken by the teacher referred to in the first chapter of this book, who prayed throughout the summer holidays to clear her mental vision of a previously troublesome girl.

Children too can be taught to stick with their prayers and not to give up until they get an answer, even when, like the little girl who prayed for a new bicycle, the answer is, "No".

The seventh day is the sabbath of the Lord thy God.

Deuteronomy 5:14

5. Honour thy father and thy mother

He was seven years old and obviously bored with the adult conversation around him and wanted to go out. "You are not to go through that door" said his dad. The boy waited his moment till Dad's attention was elsewhere, then quietly opened the door and slipped through, but not before eye contact had been made with his dad who just continued his conversation. I just couldn't contain myself "That's fatal!" I exclaimed. Dad looked slightly abashed, "I guess I'm just lazy" was his excuse.

Obedience – the first way children learn to honour their parents – is basic to educating into the right habits of thought and action. Without obedience there is constant friction in a home, children are left in a limbo of not knowing what is expected of them and without the security of learning that right actions bring satisfaction and wrong actions bring punishment.

If children can learn obedience when they are small enough to be picked up, a lot of trouble will be saved in future years, for the child can be bodily removed from what he was doing and if necessary, dumped in his cot to cool off.

Human parents could take a few tips from the animal world where there are no delinquent children, for animals never allow their offspring to do as they please. When young animals overstep the mark, retribution is swift and never forgotten. Watch a family of big cats and note what happens if one of the cubs pesters his dad. A male lion will stand so much, but if the baby ignores the warning signs, he gets a swipe that knocks him right over – probably down to the ground from the branch of a tree.

Anti-social impulses must be subjugated and there must be a refusal to yield to self-will. It is only through the lessons of obedience that children – and adults – learn the greater lesson of doing something "because it's right". Obedience to this inner motivation is the best of all, but everyone needs to be guided in the steps along the way of achieving this goal.

There is often too much questioning about the "why's" of things. Parents feel that children must be given a reason and while this is good in its place, simplicity demands that if children learn to obey first, they can understand the reason why, later. One parent's reply to his child's incessant "Why should I?" was "You're little and dumb and I'm old and smart, so you do as I say!" Unquestioning obedience is the quickest way to get results. Good teachers know this and parents shouldn't hesitate to emulate them.

Making threats in an effort to encourage good behaviour can backfire badly. For one thing, what you are doing is working from the basis of fear, which is always shaky ground, and to act in a certain way because of fear of the consequences, isn't the best motivation. That's a bit like the driver who doesn't drink because he's afraid he might get caught, when he should be abstaining because he doesn't want to endanger the lives or safety of others.

If threats are issued which are impracticable to carry out, you get yourself into a hole, for if the threat isn't carried out, the clear message is that disobedience pays off. If there are occasions when a threat seems the best course of action, then be sure you are prepared to carry it out and AT ONCE, even if you are in a public place.

You know that real progress is being made when a child is so attuned to the voice within, that he learns that he cannot disobey. When our children attended school, they had to walk down a twisty and narrow country lane. I walked down this lane many times with them and taught them where they should cross the road before I allowed them to go without me. In later years one daughter told me "You know, it never occurred to us not to do as you said." I just replied, "Well it didn't occur to me either that you might not obey."

There are five reasons why the command to honour one's father and mother is important:

1. It makes for a more peaceful home life.

2. Respect for parents lays the foundation of respect for teachers and others in authority.

3. It lays the foundation of respect for human laws.

4. It is the early means of developing the moral sense.

5. It is only when children have learnt habits of obedience, to the moral law, that they learn to be obedient to the voice of conscience and the constant inner guidance which guides and guards us.

Children can be taught that as they are obedient, they are listening to God and this is the commandment's higher meaning – that children be aroused to sensitivity to the inner voice. As young people grow to adulthood, human parents are with them less and less, but their divine Parent is never absent. The voice of God is the voice of unfailing purity and goodness and never leads into the temptations of promiscuity or drugs but always delivers from evil.

It is helpful if someone other than a parent can teach this commandment to children, but it becomes devoid of meaning unless parents give children something that they can love, respect and trust. A sad memorial to the disobedience of too many adults are those horrid traffic humps which plague us all!

> Children, the right thing for you to do is to obey your parents as those whom the Lord has set over you.   Ephesians 6:1

The next three commandments, which cover the darkest and deepest of human crimes, and with the briefest wording of the lot, can be grouped together. Most people would agree that killing and stealing are wrong, but many would say that adultery is arguable. For example, no school would knowingly employ a murderer or a burglar as a schoolteacher yet adulterers are viewed as perfectly acceptable. The word "adulterer" is not used, of course, expressions like living with a partner or being in a relationship, are more acceptable. If this seventh commandment were respected to the same extent that numbers six and eight are, what an improvement it would make to the quality of countless children's lives today! Is it significant, I wonder, that this commandment was sandwiched between the other two?

6. Thou shalt not kill

To kill anyone is directly contrary to the natural inclinations of men, which is why military training includes a hardening to the task. When the natural inclinations towards kindness and compassion are properly nurtured in a child, in later years, that individual would never kill. Cruden's Bible concordance has a telling observation: "If a sullen and jealous disposition is harboured it will only require opportunity to tempt to malice and cruelty." This points to the need to counteract sullenness or jealousy by nurturing the qualities of joy and generosity in children.

Many people may feel that this commandment is irrelevant to them, because they would never kill anybody, but should the commandment be confined to its application to the taking of human life? Can one place the killing of men in a separate category from the slaughter of animals? Tolstoy (a vegetarian) once observed that as long as we have slaughterhouses, we will have wars, which is really saying that the whole concept of killing is repugnant.

Parents should ensure that their children are not influenced into disregard for the lives of reptiles or birds. If insects or vermin must be killed, it is best to explain to a child why this must be done and to dispatch it quickly. Giving a boy fly spray to "play" with is setting him on the wrong course.

I once visited a Field Study Centre for schoolchildren where there was a notice by a vivarium, which read "Handle insects carefully, they are easily damaged". The supervisor told me that she considered that it was important to teach children a reverence for life in its simpler forms. Even the smallest child can be taught not to stamp on an ant deliberately or squash a beetle.

There is also a totally different perspective on this commandment. What about not killing off another's joy by belittling their achievements, downgrading their appearance or pooh-poohing their jokes? Young children respond well to being taught the commandment in this way and the list could go on. How often has a thoughtless word ruined someone's day?

Violence shall no more be heard in thy land.   Isaiah 60:18

7. Thou shalt not commit adultery

Nothing to do with children?

I believe that this commandment has great relevance to the lives of children, firstly, because their lives are adversely affected by adultery (and its old-fashioned cousin, fornication) and secondly because there are simple applications of the principle involved which can and should be part of a child's upbringing.

If we are to reach to the root of the problem of adultery, we have to look at the mental factors. In his Sermon on the Mount, Jesus pointed out the hidden mental cause of infidelity when he said, "Whosoever looketh on a woman to lust after her hath committed adultery with her already in his heart." (Matthew 5:28)

The thought is ever further to the deed and adultery must be stopped in the heart if its transitory attraction is to he challenged. Here the word "passion" comes to mind. The root meaning of the word "passion" is "to suffer, or allow" and denotes a mental state of being subjected to an external agent or influence. Adultery is transmitted through passive acceptance of the present mentally polluted atmosphere which does not sway the more morally robust. Even the most clandestine sexual activity, which is outside the moral law (marriage) adds to the pollution.

Unrestrained sexual indulgence has repeated itself through history and needs to be challenged in the confines of one's own heart. A wife who was in an unhappy marriage found herself the focus of attention of a married colleague at her work place and was attracted to him, too. Despite her unhappy marriage, she wished to be faithful to her wedding vows and she recognised that the physical attraction she was feeling needed to be addressed mentally. She was familiar with the biblical statement, "I know the thoughts that I think towards you, saith the Lord, thoughts of peace, and not of evil. . . ." (Jeremiah 29:11). Feeling confident that the thoughts that resulted in an immoral physical attraction could not be from God, she rejected them, and mentally demanded that they should leave her alone. The story had a happy ending, for the physical attraction did leave her and in due course of time she and her husband regained the happiness they had thought was lost.

When a couple marry, they make a solemn promise that they will forsake all others and be faithful to their spouse. This is the way of true freedom as this woman found, for there is no real satisfaction in cheating the one who trusts you and breaking your promise to him/her.

William Rees-Mogg once wrote an excellent article in the Times called, *Adultery versus Duty.* He said, "Adultery weakens the bond which allows marriage to survive natural difficulties; it is the matrimonial equivalent of an attack on the immune system, and opens the way to many other diseases. Adultery is a powerful social solvent. It tends to wash away the cement of marriage; those who depend on the stability of marriage suffer great damage as a result." The truth of his words is very plain to see, especially as it relates to the wellbeing and behaviour of children.

As with so many things, the basic teaching connected with this commandment can begin very young. Children need to be taught what a promise is – Scout and Guide promises are helpful here – and they should be taught that when you promise to do something you must do it and if you aren't sure you can do it, you don't promise. They should be taught that when they do keep promises, they will be trusted. Parents should keep promises to their children and use such instances as examples for the children. Children should be brought up to do in little things what they will be expected to do in big things later on. Older children can also be taught the value of purity and that to adulterate something is to pollute it.

Infidelity should not be condoned, but an atmosphere of admiration for restraint and faithfulness should be encouraged. If this commandment were acknowledged to be as important as those before and after, it would do more than any other one thing to stabilise society and improve the lot of countless children. There would be less crime and violence, fewer suicides and there would be less pressure on both the health and social services.

whoso committeth adultery with a woman lacketh understanding.

Proverbs 6:32

8. Thou shalt not steal

Sharing is a valuable concept for small children to learn. They can share their toys with little friends and learn to give back what has been shared with them. This builds respect for another's property and will reinforce a small child's instinctive feelings that to take something that is not yours is wrong. If a child has taken something that is not his, then it is well to be sure you understand the circumstances – was there some misunderstanding that needs correcting? Did the child know full well what he was doing, in which case it needs pointing out that he wouldn't like it if someone took his things, therefore he must not take other people's things (the Golden Rule). Whatever is said must be said with the aim of awakening the desire not to repeat the offence.

Theft by children is not confined to those who come from poor homes and are in need. Wealthy children steal when they have been brought up to believe that they can have whatever they want — they find it hard to accept that there are some things they can't have because they belong to other people. In today's affluent times many children think they can keep the mobile phone they found on the school bus because whoever lost it can easily afford to buy another.

Honesty in children depends on whether parents practise and teach honesty. Double standards by parents have debilitating effects on children. Tax evasion and collecting dole whilst working are two of the most common forms of stealing committed by people who would never class themselves as thieves.

Too many people think that it's clever to avoid paying tax, or that defrauding the government's purse is such a drop in the ocean that it doesn't matter. Then there are those who obtain quotations from firms that they have no intention of employing. Are you tempted when the man who has done some work on your house says, "Pay me cash if you like, then I needn't add the VAT"?

A builder who had done a substantial amount of work for a friend of mine offered him this sort of deal, but he picked the wrong man. "If I pay you cash," said my friend, "that would be cheating – it's dishonest. I'd be encouraging you to build your business on a dishonest practice and that's not a sound basis for any business. I couldn't do that to your business." He insisted on having a proper invoice and paying the several hundred pounds extra to an astonished builder.

Subtler forms of theft are taking a day off work when, with a bit more effort, one could go in, or avoiding hard work when one is at work. Either of these practices is effectively stealing time from an employer. Children steal time when they keep others waiting and disobedient children steal time from their classmates when the teacher has to stop the lesson to discipline them.

And now check these out:

"I don't think taking the odd stamp, envelope or phone call could be called stealing. After all it's not like breaking into somebody's home or robbing a bank."

"I travel quite often without a ticket. They can afford it, can't they?"

"Once I kept a purse I'd found. I was broke at the time."

Thieving has consequences beyond the act of stealing, for when theft takes place within a community an atmosphere of suspicion takes over.

Children therefore not only need to have it clearly spelled out that stealing is wrong, they need to be aware of the wider consequences of theft and they need the adults around them to believe it is wrong to steal and to practise what they preach.

> The man who cheats in the little things will cheat in the big things too.   Luke 16:10, J.B. Phillips

9. Thou shalt not bear false witness against thy neighbour

Taken at its face value this commandment is an instruction to take care that what we say about another is accurate, in other words, Don't tell lies about other people. It instructs us to be truthful, and to be ready to give another the benefit of the doubt. But the commandment can mean more than that. For instance, if a child has done something wrong, does that make him a bad child? Not really, for one undesirable act does not change the child's innate goodness. The distinction needs to be made between a *naughty child*, and a good child who did a *naughty thing*. In this case, we should still love the good, and mentally separate the bad from the child. It's back to looking through that yellow cellophane and seeing the blue car.

The commandment can also go beyond what we say to what we *think*. If we are thinking about others unkindly, can we expect them to think kindly about us? There is a story that Mrs. A was always being catty about Mrs. B. Mrs. C heard some of these catty remarks and wanted to do something to improve the situation, so she commented to Mrs. A, "It's funny you should say that, for Mrs. B always speaks so kindly about you!" The cattiness stopped forthwith! Never miss an opportunity to praise someone, to express gratitude for what they've done or to say something nice about them, for it works wonders.

Children who grow up in an environment with no gossip about, or criticism of, others, will themselves be less quick to criticise.

> For he that will love life, and see good days, let him refrain his tongue from evil. . . .   I Peter 3:10

10. Thou shalt not covet

The mail shot from the car dealer read "Think how jealous your friends will be when they see your new Toyota. . . ." I wrote back and said that I loved my friends and would not wish to cause them unhappiness. True affection rejoices in another's good and doesn't covet.

Children would benefit immeasurably if adult attitudes towards being "one up" could be changed. They feel it keenly when their friends have more expensive trainers, bikes and roller blades, especially when their "friends" rub this in. There is little to be gained from being miserable because of what you don't have, a fact which I once pointed out to a miserable granddaughter. She wanted a mobile phone because her friends had one. "OK," I said, "They've got phones and you haven't. You can't get one today. (Agreed, for she couldn't go into town) The rest of the day is before you and its up to you. Are you going to be miserable or happy for the rest of the day?" A simple antidote for envy that helps no end is gratitude for what one has.

It is said that Hitler's mother indulged his every whim – whatever he desired, she got it for him. Just suppose she had been firmer with him and brought him up not to covet the possessions of others, but to be grateful for what he had, what a difference that could have made to history.

Coveting is not confined to things. How about one sleepless spouse being angry when the other is peacefully slumbering? How about feeling hurt if one is excluded from a particular social gathering?

There is an interesting footnote to this commandment: In the Caucasian mountains, in the region of Nagorna-Karabakh many people live very long lives, sometimes reaching the age of 150 to 160 years old and their faculties and memory are good. A study of the life and customs of these centenarians revealed that they are not envious peoples and noted that in general people who are long-lived, tend to be satisfied with their lives.

A sound heart is the life of the flesh: but envy the rottenness of the bones.   Proverbs 14:30

After Moses had presented the Ten Commandments to the Children of Israel, there was greater harmony amongst them. The commandments worked for them and they still work today. Obedience to the commandments lifts one up the moral ladder, and leads to a more rewarding lifestyle.

Here is how the moral ladder works with stealing used as an example. You could read it for different aspects by substituting killing, committing adultery, coveting etc. (Please read from the bottom upwards)

3   The man who can't steal because the inner voice won't let him. He is responding to spiritual law.

2   The man who doesn't steal because he is obeying the moral or civil law.

1   The man who steals. His motivation is solely physical.

It is at stage 3 of the moral ladder that true freedom is found – a state which can only be fully appreciated by those who have attained that third stage, just as it is only those who have climbed to the summit of a mountain who can appreciate the view from the top.

When reverence for and joy in the commandments are established in the minds of children and young people by those who sincerely believe in their value, youngsters feel more comfortable with themselves. One doesn't feel genuinely comfortable when one is consumed with envy (No. 10) if one has little regard for one's parents (No 5) or if one spends one's time spreading ill-founded gossip (No 9) etc.

Jesus was once asked to pass judgement on the commandments and say which was the greatest. His two-fold reply was not only a neat summary, but it established the need for compassion, instead of harsh retribution when the commandments are not obeyed. He said:

Love God and love your neighbour as yourself.

To illustrate who a neighbour is, Jesus told the parable of the Good Samaritan – the man who went to the aid of an injured man after others had left him to die at the side of the road. It was significant that Jesus made the fictitious helper a Samaritan, for the Jews generally "had no dealings with the Samaritans" indicating that we are to help others in need irrespective of who they are. So go for it, love what is good with all your heart and soul and mind! Remember these commandments, obey them yourself and cherish them. Teach them to your children and so help them to discover that they truly are the rules of happiness.

Have reverence for God, and obey his commands, because this is all that man was created for.   Ecclesiastes 12:13 GBN

VI. Dealing with Drugs and Sex

Sensualism is not bliss but bondage. Whatever enslaves man is opposed to the divine government.   Mary Baker Eddy

Parents have to tell their kids that drug use is wrong and that premarital sex is wrong. We've had enough moral relativism. We have to tell kids "It's wrong. Don't do it." Colin Powell

As a society we have an unhealthy preoccupation with the body and this has a debilitating effect upon the minds of our children as they grow to adulthood. Sex, drug taking and violence, all involve the body – violence aims to inflict pain on the body and both sex and drugs aim to get pleasure and satisfaction from it. All these activities are motivated by thinking about "me" – what *I* want – in a word, self-gratification.

Self-gratification opposes the qualities previously discussed; it encourages withdrawal from social responsibility, works against good relationships and it draws us away from our unity with God, or good. This was well understood by the Nazis who actively encouraged pornography and sexual perversions as part of their campaign to weaken the mentality of the masses and make them more susceptible to manipulation. The danger in western societies today lies in the move to accord sexual excesses and deviations the status of normality and respectability and this weighs heavily upon our young people.

At a meeting once held in Boston, U.S.A. to address problems of violence and substance abuse in the area, the dean of Northeastern University School of Law in the city, stated, "We like to refer to youth offenders as 'the lost generation.' They are not lost. The reality is that we have turned off the social and spiritual lights and they can't find their way in the dark. Therefore, they are reaching for whatever they can get their hands on to, that they can find meaning in life. When you reach in the dark, you never know what you will find. Too many are finding drugs and violence. Although those things don't help to turn on the lights, they at least allow them to make it through the night. . . ."

The dean went on to say, "We will never he able to reach out fully to those in need unless we tap into the spiritual power that all of us possess and that is lying dormant in those we want to help."

These sentiments, so similar to those of Father Flanagan, point again to the need to regard those who have fallen prey to current mores as God's children with that basic goodness waiting to be re-activated. Despite all the challenges, that dormant spiritual power is being reactivated in some striking ways.

Jackie Pullinger, an ardent Christian, has done inspired work to lift addicts out of the scourge of drugs, and that too, in the most challenging of situations. Her work in Hong Kong's Walled City is legendary. The Walled City is "a place of prostitution and pornography, extortion and fear . . . yet, as [Jackie] spoke of Jesus Christ, brutal Triad gangsters were converted, prostitutes quit, and Jackie discovered a new treatment for drug addiction: baptism in the Holy Spirit." (To quote from the cover of her book, *Chasing the Dragon*). I once met a girl who had worked with Jackie Pullinger and I was deeply impressed by her confirmation of the book's message of hope and encouragement proving the fallacy of the belief that once drugs get a hold on you, you are powerless to quit. Never accept this. That inner voice of the Holy Spirit is there for everyone and the desire for freedom is a prayer that will be answered.

One young man who had been involved in violence and drug dealing for years told how he suddenly became aware of this voice, "I was in an alley selling marijuana to a guy, and I heard a voice telling me to stop. I turned around, thinking somebody was there. The guy says, 'Hey, c'mon, you going to sell me the stuff or not?' I heard the voice again telling me I was doing bad things to people. I wasn't on drugs or drunk. I started to cry, and I knew I had to stop dealing." Another young man who was addicted to alcohol, tobacco and marijuana had long discussions with a friend who was free from all these habits. The friend's good example came to have a great influence on his life and the motivation to be free of all drugs came when he recognised a great truth:

Drugs are a major obstacle to independent thinking.

This realisation gave him the desire and the strength to reject this imposition on his mental freedom. The desire for freedom from the domination of sensualism, is key to retaining or gaining that dominion.

A man who was brought up in a permissive environment and who had indulged in numerous sexual relationships was introduced to the idea that divine help was available to him in his search for a deeper satisfaction. His awakening came when he realised that there were only four basic things he needed to survive physically – eat, drink, eliminate and sleep. He realised that he had a choice about sex – that it wasn't an absolute necessity to his existence and this helped him in gaining his freedom from sexual obsessions.

Then there is the tricky question of homosexuality, a practice which, since Old Testament times has commonly been regarded as unnatural. We read in the book of Leviticus, (18:22) "Thou shalt not lie with mankind as with womankind: it is an abomination." We need to ask, why should homosexuality arouse intuitive feelings of revulsion in so many people if it is normal and right? For understandable personal reasons, we hear little about individuals who have practised homosexuality for a period and, when they stopped, felt a sense of relief, frequently coupled with repugnance for what they had been doing. One individual who was courageous enough to share his experience, wrote, "During my teenage years I believed that I was homosexual and practised homosexual activities. Progressively my whole life became affected. School, career and social interactions all suffered because of what I now consider immoral and unethical behaviour. I felt handcuffed, embarrassed, and dependent upon momentary pleasures of the body. For eleven years I struggled along, feeling desperately alone with the problem and having no one to turn to."

This young man eventually began to ponder the implications of being a child of God which, in his words again, "began to free [him] from the misconception that [he] was a physical puppet governed and controlled by false appetites and pleasures."

He concluded, "One day I simply felt free! It was a wonderful feeling. I had lost all desire for homosexual relationships. I was free. I thanked God for releasing me from the grip that had seemed to hold me physically, emotionally and mentally." This man is now happily married and his story is told in the book, *Healing Spiritually*. Even one instance like the forgoing should make us pause and consider this whole question carefully, for if one person felt that release from homosexuality was a freedom, surely there must be many others who have felt the same? As with so many ambivalent situations, it does help to separate the act from the person and, whilst not condoning the act, to treat the person with compassion and respect.

The above instances illustrate the might of that power which lies within us all to overcome the impulses of a physically based mentality. It is of inestimable value when children are brought up to feel close to God and to feel His purity and love, for it is a protection from physically based temptations. One young woman who had enjoyed this advantage as a child, was strengthened by it when faced with the threat of rape. She recounted her experience as follows:

When I was a teenager I was far from home once, and trying to get to the house of some friends without any money, I unwisely accepted a ride from a man, who, as soon as I got in, took off down a side country road that led into mountains where very few people lived. He was very drunk, and immediately began grabbing me all over and telling me he was going to rape me.

I had been taught ...that God made each of us in His likeness and that God's creation is good, not destructive: that God's love was always with me, protecting me, and governing even strangers like this man.

So I began talking to him, telling him that he was God's child, that God loved both of us and was constantly caring for us; that His love was satisfying and never brought suffering. I was not afraid of the man's threats nor of the fact that he was touching me, because I had seen evidence of God's power to heal and protect often enough when I was growing up not to doubt that God loved this man as much as me and would guide him, too.

Soon the man stopped touching me and became sober. When I was quiet for a moment he asked me to continue talking because he loved what he was hearing. We talked for some time. When we finally came upon a small cafe (the first building we had seen since entering the road), he stopped, took me inside, and asked me for the telephone number of the place where I was headed. He called my friends and asked them to come and get me. Then he thanked me for what I had shared with him and left.

In that remarkable experience, the girl's understanding of God's presence was sufficient to enable her to treat her would-be attacker with a compassion that melted away the man's carnal intentions. Carnal-mindedness is no match for the power of prayer when properly brought to bear upon a situation, for prayer has the vitality to awaken people from the mesmerism of physicality.

Young people who are brought up with strong moral and spiritual values are better equipped to withstand today's myriad temptations. Westerners can learn something here from young Asians whose respect for the value systems of their culture gives them mental strength. "The only virgins I know in this university are all Asians" one student told me. Too many students from the west have lost more than their virginity, for they have grown up in a society that marginalises the spiritual dimension of life.

Adolescents have lost their way because we have allowed traditional values to be tossed out of the window with nothing positive with which to replace them. The 'anything goes' philosophy does not replace anything. According to an American study undertaken early in 2002, teens want stronger parenting. The teens themselves suggested that parents should enforce curfew rules and stay up till they return home. They want parents to initiate conversations about tough decisions. They want their parents to call their friends' parents to make sure they are being supervised when they are away from home. Furthermore they want parents to enforce consequences when rules are broken. We must not fail these youngsters; we must heed what they say, take a good look at what we've done and CHANGE THINGS with respect to both drugs and sex. The rest of this chapter presents some tough options which get to the root of the problems.

> Flee the evil desires of youth, and pursue righteousness, faith, love and peace. . . .   II Timothy 2:22 NIV

The Mask of Respectability

> Alcohol is a factor in the causation of crime, mental illness, road accidents and family breakdown. Every year it kills, maims and disables thousands, ruining the lives of the victims, their family and friends. But unfortunately drinking has become so much a part of every social occasion that we hardly think about the colossal damage it causes.   Lord Avebury

I do not see any "quick fix" for the problem of drug taking, but I do believe there is a very simple long-term solution. It is one, however that will not be popular.

According to national surveys, one in four people aged 16 to 29 has used illegal drugs, and heroin accounts for £1.3 billion of property crimes, committed by addicts to finance their addiction. Responsible adults see the problem of illegal drugs as something they deplore, as a habit with which they would never wish to be associated and they are shocked when a teenager dies after taking an ecstasy tablet. Many young people on the other hand see recreational drugs as an aid to being sociable with their friends, to loosening their inhibitions, for getting a "kick", experiencing a "high", for forgetting their troubles for a time or even for solving their problems.

We should ask ourselves why the young should have this view. Drug culture did not suddenly arise from nowhere.

Drug culture arose from the public acceptance of legal drugs, especially alcohol

Drug taking has grown as an extension of the tobacco and alcohol habits, for 63% of 12-15 year old regular smokers have tried drugs, yet only 1% of those who have never smoked or drunk alcohol have tried drugs. The dangers of tobacco smoking are now widely recognised, whilst the more widespread problems of alcohol are largely ignored because alcohol is given a mask of respectability, yet as noted by Lord Avebury, alcohol is linked to more social harm than any other drug. Alcohol is behind an estimated 15 per cent of acute admissions to hospital and is a factor in up to 30 per cent of accidents, furthermore it costs the National Health Service around £3 billion a year. Despite these sobering facts, children are brainwashed, often from a very early age, into accepting the consumption of alcohol as a normal way of life.

Consuming alcohol whilst bemoaning the use of other recreational drugs, must surely rate as the worst example of double standards that there has ever been, anytime, anywhere. It is safe to say that if adults did not drink alcohol, the next generation would not be taking other drugs, for the motives for taking illegal drugs are the same as those for drinking alcohol (please check above) it is only that the substance being used is different.

Can it seriously be imagined that if alcohol were being introduced today that we would agree to its legalisation when the harm it causes is far in excess of the harm caused by all the illegal drugs put together and when most crimes of violence occur under its influence? If you doubt this, just do a survey of your local paper for a month and check how much trouble in your community is linked with alcohol consumption. Such a survey would make a good topic for a school project.

Drinking alcohol is such a deeply engrained social custom that it is not challenged as it should be. All those who condone the use of alcohol share responsibility for the present drug culture. If you drink and your son grows up to take crack cocaine, you share a degree of responsibility. Every social drinker, by his actions, is paving the way for others to succumb to drunkenness, alcoholism and illegal drug taking.

Many people expressed concern when alcopops (drinks dressed like soft drinks, yet which contain some alcohol) were introduced into Britain in 1995. By 1997 youngsters were spending an estimated £700,000 a day on these drinks, bought mainly from supermarkets. Iceland and the Co-op showed some social responsibility by banning alcopops, but other groups did not follow their lead. At Sainsbury's Annual Meeting, held in July 1997, John Beasley, a concerned London social worker asked this question, "Alcopops are causing increasing concern. A school was burnt down by a fourteen-year old boy after he had drunk alcopops. Another fourteen-year old boy died after falling under the wheels of a train while under the influence of alcohol in alcopops. As one of the company's objectives is 'to contribute to the public good and to the quality of life in the community' can we have an assurance that as from today no more alcopops will he sold in any Sainsbury store?" That assurance was not given and Sainsbury's and most other big supermarkets continue to act as though profits are more important than people.

When sixteen children are killed by a gunman the whole country is in an uproar, so why does the same populace calmly ignore the five hundred plus people killed every year by drunken drivers? (a total of well over 5,000 children, men and women during the 1990s) How is it that when a seven-year old is raped by a drunken man, that no action is taken to remove the cause of such abuse? Why do children's charities ask for help to rebuild children's lives that have been blighted by drunken parents, yet have no plans to tackle the cause of these outrages? It is like removing the cobwebs and leaving the spiders.

The anti-smoking lobby is so strong, that one might wonder why, if alcohol is such an evil, is there not more organised opposition to its use? The answer is twofold. Firstly as the vast majority of the population are drinkers, with, it seems, an especially high concentration amongst those in high places, they are reluctant to forgo a habit that they believe to be pleasurable. MP's have their photos taken in their local pub with a beer in their hand to show how in touch with the public they are and when a Chancellor of the Exchequer announces "There will be no increase in the tax on alcohol in this budget," take note of the cheers that echo through the House.

The other reason why opposition to alcohol is lacking lies in the fact that the damage caused by alcohol is so widespread, varying from violent or accidental deaths to vomit spewed out on the pavement or carpet. The trouble caused by smoking on the other hand, is confined to one area, namely health, and therefore opposition is spearheaded by the powerful British Medical Association.

Alcohol is the main cause of a significant proportion of unwanted pregnancies, it is the main cause of football hooliganism with its harm to people, property and our country's reputation, it is the reason why cities are unsafe at night; it is why many women get battered and countless homes broken. Damage is not caused just by the drunkards and the alcoholics, but also by moderate drinkers who have had just a bit too much. And a high proportion of the harm is done, not to the drinker, but to those who are on the receiving end of the drinker's loss of decency and good sense. A friend of mine who had a drunken father said that as a child she never wanted presents for Christmas, all she wished for was that her dad wouldn't be drunk.

When illegal drugs first became news, I went to a meeting about drug taking amongst the young. Everyone went to learn something about this new phenomenon which was, we thought, something with which we were totally unfamiliar. The speaker soon disillusioned everybody. "Hands up those who take sleeping tablets." "Do you ever use pain killers?" We have become a society that all too often seeks solace and relief by popping a pill into the mouth and these questions made folks realise that this was not an issue that could be completely isolated from their own practice of taking drugs for medicinal purposes.

Most school programmes aimed at preventing drug use appear to be woefully inadequate. Endeavouring to instil fear of the consequences is usually the main approach. This method has failed to work before and it is failing now. "I couldn't wait to try ecstasy" said one teenager after the police had visited her school as part of a drugs prevention programme, which if it did nothing else, certainly educated the pupils in what different drugs are available, what they look like and how they are administered.

How shall we ever hope to eradicate this terrible problem while we continue to separate illegal from legal drugs? We need to look to those who are completely free from the use of recreational drugs for answers as they are the only group who are 100% sure of never becoming addicts. Those who enjoy an alcohol-free life-style would commonly describe their approach not in terms of having to give up something, but as having found something better. Ask these people why they don't drink and the replies are likely to include the fact that they prefer to remain in control of their thinking, their bodies and their actions. A thoughtful (and very popular) young university student put her decision to stay alcohol-free very simply; she said, "I couldn't see that alcohol could do anything for me."

Non drinkers are not impressed by the argument that you need alcohol to have a good time, simply because they know its not true. The belief that you need something from WITHOUT to give you enjoyment, is an illusion that can never fool those who have already discovered that the capacity for joy is to be found WITHIN. I have a witty and outgoing friend who likes to tell the story of when she and her husband were at a large party and towards the end of the evening, someone said to her "I just don't understand it, you're the liveliest one here and you haven't touched a drop."

To help the young find that inner satisfaction and to arouse the desire to keep control of their thoughts, bodies and actions, can be the only long-term way to combating the use of drugs and how can this be done by those who are themselves indulging? Your consciousness is your most precious possession, and no one really wants to yield up their most valuable asset. Cherishing your own thinking is a life-long lesson and children must learn how to guard their thinking against unwanted intrusion. When you say, "No thank you, I don't smoke," or "I don't drink," you are under no obligation to give a reason. One wit who did give a reason, said, "I don't drink because I want to know when I'm having a good time."

A woman who had been brought up to be a non drinker found it tough going but stuck with it because she could clearly see how frequently the allure of alcohol led to addiction. When her eldest son was growing to maturity she gave the whole question some serious thinking. She suggested to him that when he encountered the problems, not only of tobacco and alcohol, but also of drugs, instead of holding back and hoping someone else would say, "No thank you" she suggested that he should be the first to speak out, for there would probably be others in the group who wanted to say no, but for one reason or another were afraid to do so.

She told her son that if he passed without hesitation, others would probably follow and that was exactly what happened. Several friends told him later that his decision gave them the courage to say no and they were grateful to him.

Most youngsters start drinking solely because of the social pressure and during the 1980s, there were a number of initiatives to provide alcohol-free clubs for young people. One, which attracted a great deal of publicity at the time, was the Parrot and Palm Club in Worthing. It was organised by two dedicated social workers and I was invited to the official opening by the local MP. I was so impressed by what I saw. The young people there took great pride in the place, the atmosphere was terrific and the drinks were sophisticated. It demonstrated very well that you don't need alcohol to have a good time, especially now there are so many suitable alternatives available. Sadly it closed after the social workers that ran it moved out of the area.

An organisation which produces literature ostensibly to combat the troubles caused by alcohol consumption, is funded by the breweries. The Portman Group is a wolf in sheep's clothing. Their recommendations suggest introducing children to drinking in the atmosphere of the home where they can be properly educated into what they are pleased to call "sensible drinking", ignoring the fact that it is so-called sensible drinking that starts countless thousands off on the road to becoming immoderate drinkers. I would recommend the literature put out by Hope UK (www. hopeuk.org) as being more realistic in its approach.

Every binge drinker started off as a social drinker.

Parents would be well advised to note and ponder the close links between violence, lust and drink and then make an informed decision about "sensible drinking".

The influence of the alcohol lobby is such that wine is the only substance for human consumption that is exempt from the requirement to state its ingredients on the label. Wine, which has such a carefully orchestrated image of sophistication, should be deprived of its mystique and children should be told what it really is – grape juice gone bad. The reality of some wines are far from the image in the advertisements. A reputable German wine producer told me that unscrupulous producers put all sorts of rubbish into their wine. People don't want to know this, but some of us remember the Austrian company who "enhanced" the flavour of their wine with anti-freeze.

Before non-alcoholic drinks were as extensively distributed as they are now, I was involved in their marketing, which took me to exhibitions organised by breweries for their customers, mostly publicans. I remember speaking to one landlord and his wife, trying to encourage them to increase their range of safe drinks for drivers. "How would you feel if one of your customers drove off from your pub and killed someone?" I asked them. The publican shrugged off the question and muttered "It'd be his own fault, wouldn't it?" but the point went home with his wife. She looked horrified, "I'd feel terrible," she said, wide-eyed. She had obviously never thought through the implications before.

Drinking alcohol can be compared to a raging fire. Fire needs three things in order to get a hold. It needs fuel, it needs igniting and it needs oxygen in order to keep burning. Alcohol is the fuel for drinking which is ignited by advertising, but it is the social acceptance that provides the atmosphere which keeps it going. Islam is presently the world's fastest growing religion, yet it bans the consumption of alcohol. Isn't this an indication of what a practical help it is to remove the atmosphere of social acceptance? Responsible people should be doing much more to deny alcohol its "oxygen". Abstinence is not a deprivation; drinking is the deprivation – it deprives you of your dignity and of your ability to make sound judgements.

If you are a drinker, ask yourself "How can I consent to being part of a culture which is causing so much misery and heartbreak?" "How can I indulge for the sake of such flimsy motives as 'I like the taste'?" "Shouldn't I have more unselfish motivation for my life?"

If you are a parent, ask yourself, "How can I speak honestly to my children about the dangers of drug taking if I am indulging in the same type of habit myself?" "Isn't the principle the same whether the substance used is a legal or an illegal drug?" "How can I tell my children to keep in control of their thinking and their bodies, if I am yielding my mentality to alcohol?"

Horatius Bonar, a founder member of the Free Kirk of Scotland stated that "Total abstinence is the only unmistakable protest against drink." Would that we had many more who would register that unmistakable protest! We should promote an atmosphere where voluntary abstinence from all non-medical drugs becomes cool, where an alcohol free lifestyle is looked upon with admiration and where this wretched mask of respectability is removed.

Wine is a mocker, strong drink is raging; and whosoever is deceived thereby is not wise.   Proverbs 20:1

Sex – Is it Love or Lust?

Marriage remains a basic building block of any society and the surest foundation of a secure family life   Dr. George Carey

If two people love each other, then there is no reason why they shouldn't live together, is a widely held sentiment. But what is meant by that word "love"? Would the sentence have the same meaning if it read, "Two people who are physically attracted to each other"? as opposed to, "Two people, a man and a woman, who are devoted to promoting the happiness and welfare of each other"? I submit that the first is lust and the second is love and that they can be totally different. The reason they get confused, is due to the fact that both contribute to that delightfully happy state called being in love. We use the word "love" for so many different meanings; we have one word in English where the ancient Greeks had four and as a result, the word love is overused and underrated. Loving books, for example, does not have the same connotation as loving one's child, and erotic love, the physical attraction which may be completely lacking in affection, should properly be called lust.

Lust takes us back to self-gratification whereas love promotes the welfare of others. Lust is selfishness; love is unselfishness. Lust tends to monopolise your life, focussing on the object of your desire, to the detriment of other activities; love is outgoing and freeing. Love is fulfilling; lust always craves for more because it is not truly satisfying. Love brings us closer to God and lust separates us from Him.

Experience tells us that it is love and not lust that lays a sure foundation for a happy marriage. Clues to what does lay a good foundation for an enduring partnership can be found by reading some of the comments that appear in the local paper when couples who have been married for fifty or even sixty years are asked the secrets of their happiness. I've never read one that said, "It was our fantastic sex life that kept us together." They more commonly cite "lots of give and take" "readiness to forgive" and "sharing a sense of humour". The best motive I ever heard for getting married was from a young husband who said, "We knew we could do more good in the world as a couple than we would do separately."

Such comments hint at an enduring love that puts another's welfare before one's own, which cares for those in need and which labours to draw out the good in others. Peter Ustinov once said that "Love is an act of endless forgiveness". True love forgives and forgets for true love is caring compassion for others. Its origin is in the impartial, universal and unchanging Love which is God. It is poured forth to all, irrespective of race, colour or creed and is broad enough to awaken the conscience of men and to empower them to do good. This is the love that holds a marriage together. Love is a vast concept and consideration of its component parts helps us to understand more of what it implies. St. Paul's brilliant analysis of love in his epistle written to the Corinthians (Chapter 13) does just this and what Paul said has been clarified by Henry Drummond in his outstanding little book, *The Greatest Thing in the World*. Professor Drummond was a distinguished 19th century Scotsman who made a special study of the relationship between Science and Christianity and he set out St. Paul's ideas like this:

ST. PAUL	HENRY DRUMMOND
"Love suffereth long"	Patience
"And is kind"	Kindness
"Love envieth not"	Generosity
"Love vaunteth not itself, is not puffed up."	Humility
"Doth not behave itself unseemly"	Courtesy
"Seeketh not her own"	Unselfishness
"Is not easily provoked"	Good temper
"Thinketh no evil"	Guilelessness (Honesty)
"Rejoiceth not in iniquity, but rejoiceth in the truth."	Sincerity

The Corinthians were a lascivious lot and Paul obviously felt they needed help in understanding what real love was all about instead of being deceived by the lust that they possibly mistook for love. Young people today need this guidance every bit as much as the young people in Corinth did to help them understand the distinction between love and lust. In modern times, the rot of confusion set in during the 1960s. Listen to pre-sixties love songs and they were filled with tenderness, romance and love. Listen to today's pop offerings and the tenderness, romance and love have all but vanished to be replaced by sex, sex and more sex.

I'm not sure now when "making love" was phased out and became "having sex" but it is symptomatic of the belief that the union of a man and a woman is physical. It is strange that we use the word "sex" to indicate a union, when the root meaning of the word is separation. Emphasis on the physical aspects of a boy/girl relationship has deprived the young of the innocent fun when just holding hands was really exciting. The first kisses were of a tentative nature and not for sexual arousal – there was ample time for that later. The more gentle approach gave time for sharing experiences, enjoying jokes and exploring mutual interests which was a far better preparation for marriage should the relationship develop in that direction. Hopping into bed straight away makes something mundane that should be special, and eventually takes away the great fun of a honeymoon when sexual intercourse is all the more exciting because it is a first and anticipation maximises the attraction. It is time more people spoke up to tell the young what they are missing through promiscuity.

One pathetic little 13 year old who appeared on a television discussion about sexual activity amongst teenagers said her reaction at the end of her first experience was "Is that all it is? Is that it?" Society, aided by the media, has degraded an act which should be the outcome of genuine love and trust and turned it into a lustful, and too often, joyless exercise devoid of anything but physical indulgence. But such is the nature of sexual involvement, that once you have indulged, it becomes increasingly tempting to continue, and this poor child went on experimenting in a vain attempt to discover some wonderful sensation that she ignorantly believed to be solely physical.

Even very young children are having their precious innocence eroded in our sexually saturated society where we hear so much about lust in the guise of love and so little about genuine affection, and this is having grave consequences. The chairman of a group investigating the breakdown of family life and moral values said, "Civilisations have broken up in the past and we cannot be complacent that ours will not."

Human sexual activity has always needed certain restraints. We have laws that prohibit bigamy and polygamy and laws that define the age of consent for sex and marriage. The motives for such laws have been to preserve a stable state of society and to protect the interests of children. It is because of the disruptive effects on children and the consequences of that disruption that the need to strengthen the institution of marriage is a matter of the greatest urgency.

Love and stability go hand in hand in providing the best possible environment in which to raise secure and confident children. The highest degree of love and stability can only be obtained within the framework of marriage – and ideally a marriage where there is more emphasis on the unity of compatible qualities than on the physical union of bodies.

The institution of marriage, the legal union of a man and a woman for life, has served society well over the centuries giving organisation and strength to civilisation. Marriage grew out of the desire of two individuals to raise a family together, to have an appropriate outlet for their sexual urges and to care for each other "so long as [they] both shall live." The same pattern of pairing can be observed in the animal kingdom, where some species mate for life and develop great affection for each other. It was a natural development in human society for this long-term commitment to have legal recognition.

Marriage is a legal matter and a marriage certificate is a legal document. Guests at a wedding are witnesses to the legality of the proceedings and living together outside wedlock is literally living outside the law, which is, I would imagine, why it was formerly called "living in sin".

If two people enter into a business partnership, they will normally have some form of legal agreement. Marriage is a lifetime business partnership and more. Long term stability for children is less assured if the parents themselves are not fully committed to each other. When a young man once challenged his mother, "Why bother about a marriage certificate, does it really matter?" she asked him, "Does it not mean anything to you to have had a secure home all these years because your father and I were absolutely committed to each other?" He paused. "I see what you mean," he said. Some time later he was married.

Divorce has become like a contagious disease with the virus being caught from the media and especially from television with its determination to regard both casual liaisons and any relationship outside marriage as acceptable and normal. A young man who was contemplating marriage asked his dad, "How will I know that I will never be tempted to look at another woman?" His dad, who recognised the insidious nature of current mental attitudes towards sexual laxity and the unseen effect that these can have, wisely replied that if these thoughts came to him, the son should realise that they were not really his thoughts, but solely the product of present prevailing attitudes, therefore he should firmly reject them from his consciousness and that if he was faithful in doing this, they would cease to have a hold over him.

How often does one hear the phrase "it didn't work out" as though "it" had a life of its own! When it comes to the nitty-gritty, it is the mental factors that either make or break a marriage.

Selfishness is death to a marriage; failure to think of the other spouse's point of view and unwillingness to forgive, all contribute to failures. The current emphasis on women's independence is frequently unhelpful if it is bought at the expense of understanding the need for compromises without which no marriage will succeed. It is heartening to hear of young couples who have made that legal commitment and found that it strengthened their resolve to overcome problems when otherwise they would have split up. Hopefully they also discover that commitment is not a restriction but a quality that gives purpose, fulfilment and satisfaction in life.

Young couples sometimes give financial reasons as an excuse for living together whilst unmarried and it is baffling that successive governments have gradually whittled away the financial benefits that used to accrue to married couples, whilst at the same time giving lip service to "strengthening the family." However, legal rights of co-habitees are markedly inferior to those who are married and indeed one might ask what right have unmarried couples to expect legal benefits when they have not taken the prior step of obtaining legal recognition for their union? An unmarried father has no automatic responsibility for his children – financial or otherwise – and no automatic right of access to his children if the couple separate. An abandoned wife is able to apply for child support, which may not be forthcoming for a "partner" a term I deplore because it attempts to give status to relationships that have neither legal nor moral standing. It should be remembered that legal arrangements are not made for situations where everything goes according to plan, they are a safeguard for when things go wrong.

We need more couples to work together to break the frequency of divorce and traditional values on sexuality need to be voiced much more vociferously. Human effort alone is inadequate to solve the very difficult situation in which we now find ourselves. We need help from a power greater than ourselves.

What therefore God hath joined together, let not man put asunder.

Mark 10:9

Sex Education

> We cannot solve the problems that we have created with the same
> thinking that created them.   Einstein

The current approach to sex education for teenagers is that teens are going to have sex anyway, so need instructing in the art of contraception. The result of this policy is ever-increasing teenage pregnancies and abortion to which the response always seems to be, "We need more sex education." I submit that we don't need more of the same; our approach to sex education is too narrow. We need a new approach.

In theory, sex education should be a very simple matter. Little children who don't see their parents naked and with no siblings of the opposite sex need to be told the difference between boys' and girls' bodies and that they have private parts which should be kept private. Before children start school they should be told how babies are conceived and born. This is really no big deal for small children don't find these matters of special interest and certainly don't want a long discussion on the subject.

Apart from answering the occasional questions that may arise, there is no need for anything further until the approach of puberty when both boys and girls need to be acquainted with the bodily changes they will experience. All this should be a matter for the home. In practice, it doesn't always work out to be so simple because some parents flunk the issue because of embarrassment in discussing sexual matters. Many young people are therefore left in ignorance and long-suffering schoolteachers have to help out. It is here that the whole issue has become clouded, because, to put it bluntly, sex education can focus on sex, not for procreation, but for recreation – whether straight or gay – and valuable educational time is being sucked up by programmes that are sometimes morally questionable. It is my firm belief that it is well for parents to tackle this whole question at home before it is tackled at school. It's always wise to get your spoke in first and don't wait for your children to approach you – you should be the one to introduce the topic.

A male teacher, who was given the task of taking a sex education lesson with a class of teenage boys, was unhappy to find that the approach being taken by his colleague, who was teaching the girls, was to focus on the pleasures of sex. He decided that it would be more realistic to focus on the question of responsibility and he gave what must be one of the most original sex education lessons ever, by telling the story of David and Bathsheba. We read in the Bible:

> And it came to pass in an eveningtide, that David arose from off his bed, and walked upon the roof of the king's house: and from the roof he saw a woman washing herself; and the woman was very beautiful to look upon.
>
> And David sent messengers and took her; and she came in unto him, and he lay with her.

When Bathsheba told David that she was expecting his child, he arranged the murder of Bathsheba's husband, Uriah, and then took Bathsheba to be his wife, but their child died. No enduring good came of the union, for when their second child, Solomon, eventually became king, his rule was not only the end of the dynasty, but of the kingdom, which thereafter was divided. The teacher made the point that sex outside marriage is like a stone thrown into a pond, the ripples go further and further out, and eventually the results can be devastating.

Nowhere does the Bible condone adultery, impurity or unnatural sex, nor does it ignore the need for compassion, accountability and responsibility. Why do we imagine we know better, when we look at the moral mess we are in? Can anyone honestly think that much good has come out of the present approach to sex education?

Instead of focussing on sex education, per se, schools should have a programme of education for marriage and parenting which embraces sex education and which presents abstinence as the **only** reliable option, for such programmes have been shown to reduce rates of both pregnancy and abortion.

Sex education, whether in home or school, should face the fact that so-called "safe sex" is by no means safe, for no contraceptive is 100% guaranteed and even the pill fails on occasions. Young people must be made keenly aware that many married couples experienced in contraception have unplanned pregnancies and that if they embark on sexual experiments in their teens they have the additional factor of inexperience weighing heavily against them. They also need to have it spelled out to them in no uncertain terms that when they indulge in petting that very strong emotions may be aroused which they will find difficult to handle.

A good case can be made for involving teenage mums in sex education for girls in schools. They can spell out the harsh reality of single parenthood – the financial challenges, how you feel isolated when your friends go out and you have to stay in, how your career prospects are ruined or on hold for years and the constant demands that babies and toddlers make on you. Girls also need the assurance that being a virgin won't make boys lose interest in them for experience shows that this is nothing more than an insidious myth.

We can have immense sympathy for single parents, and admire those who rise above all the odds and raise their children well, but we should at the same time condemn the public acceptance of the lower moral standards which, more than any other one factor, has brought about the state of affairs in which one parent families are such a significant section of many communities. A young woman who had been brought up by a single parent said in a radio interview, "I always wished I had a Dad and I don't know any child brought up by her Mum who didn't want her Dad."

The young need help in awakening to their God-given ability to control their bodies instead of having their bodies control them.

Motivation is key. Schoolgirls can well do without the anxiety of wondering if they are pregnant. Teens need help to think this well through; they desperately need helping to discover the security that comes from feeling inwardly comfortable with one's actions.

Here is a quiz I once used as a basis for discussion with a teenage class in Sunday School. The pupils already had a good moral grounding and the aim of the quiz was to help them to think carefully about the issues and to draw responsible conclusions. We knew each other well and I believe their answers were honest.

1. If you have sex, might it be because you think that "everybody" does? *(Yes, they said it would be)*
2. Could it indicate a lack of moral courage? *(They said yes it would)*
3. Would it be exercising any spiritual qualities? (*They knew it wouldn't*)
4. Would it be physical indulgence? *(They knew it would)*
5. No contraceptive is 100% safe.

    BOYS: Are you financially able to support a baby? *(No)*
    GIRLS: Can you face the responsibility of looking after a baby 24 hours a day? (*No*)
                Would you want the trauma (and it is a trauma) of an abortion? *(No)*

6. Does having sex help you judge the right person to marry and live with for the rest of your days? (*They thought it wouldn't*)
7. Is unselfishness a good quality? *(They knew it was)*
8. Is there any connection between unselfishness and having sex? *(They knew there wasn't)*
9. Does sex give real (permanent) satisfaction. *(They thought it wouldn't)*
10. Would God guide you to do this? *(They knew She wouldn't)*

THINK ABOUT YOUR ANSWERS TO THE ABOVE QUESTIONS, THEN ANSWER THESE:

If teens have sex:
11. Is it a good thing socially? *(No)*
12. Is it morally acceptable? *(No)*
13. Is it compatible with spirituality? *(No)*
14. Are you willing to pray 'Lead me not into temptation'? *(They said they were)*

Too many young people grow into adulthood believing that an active sex life is the ultimate fulfilment, and that it is natural to yield to lustful urges, but many celibate individuals could testify otherwise. The Dalai Lama, in his autobiography, tackles this subject straight on when speaking of his decision to become a Buddhist monk which requires a vow of celibacy, and the views that he puts forward add an important dimension to a well-balanced sex education programme. He writes:

> I am sometimes asked whether this vow of celibacy is really desirable and indeed whether it is really possible. Suffice it to say that its practice is not simply a matter of suppressing sexual desires. On the contrary, it is necessary fully to accept the existence of those desires and to transcend them by the power of reasoning. When successful, the result on the mind can be very beneficial. The trouble with sexual desire is that it is a blind desire. To say, 'I want to have sex with that person' is to express a desire which is not intellectually directed in the way that 'I want to eradicate poverty in the world' is an intellectually directed desire. Furthermore the gratification of sexual desire can only give temporary satisfaction. Thus as Nagajuna, the great Indian scholar, said:

> When you have an itch, you scratch.
> But not to have an itch at all
> Is better than any amount of scratching.

Just as refraining from retaliation when someone wants to pick a fight should be regarded as a sign of strength and something to be admired (see page 31), we need the same approach to refraining from sex when the temptation to indulge presents itself. Abstinence needs to be admired as a sign of strength and virginity needs once again to be respected in both males and females.

Is this beneficial mental state, which gives freedom from carnal desires, necessarily confined to the unmarried? No! There are many happily married couples who do not have frequent sexual intercourse – or who do not feel the need for it at all and it's an important aspect of sex education that teenagers are made aware of this. Too often it is assumed that all couples indulge in frequent sex. A young friend who confided that she and her husband went many months without having intercourse, asked me, "Do you think we're not normal?" I told her that they were quite normal, the trouble is, that it's not fashionable to say so. When a couple have a row, making love is one way of making up; conversely, when a couple experience great unity, peace and happiness together, they may not feel a need to express the unity they feel in a physical way. It is interesting to note that primitive Christians only engaged in sexual relations for the purpose of procreation. Young couples sometimes instinctively feel that they wish to refrain from lovemaking during the wife's pregnancy and the purity of their instincts can only be of benefit to their unborn child.

We are burying our heads in the sand if we don't face the unpalatable fact that during the years since sex education has been pushed as the answer to teenage pregnancies, those pregnancies have increased at an alarming rate. Youngsters need more help in knowing how to say, "No" and meaning it; also they need to understand that this is not a deprivation, but a blessing.

> Then Joseph . . . took unto him his wife: and knew her not till she had brought forth her firstborn son: and he called his name JESUS.
>
> Matthew 1:24,25

VII. The Butter and Honey Diet

> Butter and honey shall he eat, that he may know to refuse the evil, and choose the good.   Isaiah 7:15

Butter and honey represent the most pure and natural foods. Pure food for thought is needed to give young children a yardstick for future years against which to measure literature, art, music, and drama and to choose that which is wholesome, beautiful, and stimulating. If we feed confused moral images to small children before they have a proper value system in place, we are not equipping them to judge wisely in their later years.

Much attention is given to the quality of our food and certainly no responsible adult would feed food to a child that is going rotten, but are we as careful as to the nature of the food that is fed into the minds of children? Do we carefully check its suitability and quality to see that it is not rotten? A little observation and investigation shows that this is not always the case. If it were, more care would be taken not to allow impure concepts and disturbing images to enter children's thoughts and dull their sensitivity. Its not that "the world is a bad place and they'd better get used to it," but rather "We must see that the next generation is not hardened to evil, then they will work to make the world a better place."

One of the great privileges of being a parent, grandparent or teacher is having the opportunity to introduce children to the world of books, a world of fantasy creatures, from fairies, witches and pixies to robots and monsters, a world where children have amazing, incredible adventures and where animals speak and act like humans. I make no apology for the fact that I am paying more attention to books in this chapter than to any other medium.

I believe books to be tremendously important and that despite all the impact of technology, that books will continue to be of prime importance to children's development. Books are read both for enjoyment and for information or for a combination of both and the best books for children often combine both. More than any other one thing, books for children should be FUN and part of the fun for little children is in hearing a story for the umpteenth time and joyfully anticipating what is coming next. Children never tire of hearing a good story, and the frequent repetition enjoyed by children is mitigated in some degree by the fact that a really good children's book is one that adults enjoy too. Classics written by J.R.R. Tolkein, Lewis Carrol, Arthur Ransome, A.A. Milne, Beatrix Potter, Dr. Seuss and many others give endless pleasure to both adults and children.

There are plenty of good children's authors about and how needed they are when you consider for a moment all the rotten food for thought that is put before our children. Obvious examples are sex, violence, coarse language and the unpleasant ways in which one person so often treats another on TV.

Understanding something of the profound effect our thoughts have on our lives should make us consider most carefully our children's visual and intellectual environment. Which films and videos will stimulate the imagination in wholesome and lively directions and add to the child's store of useful knowledge? What toys and books will encourage a healthy mentality? The selection of toys on sale usually show a marked contrast between boys' and girls' departments. Toys for girls are all sweetness and light, but too many toys for boys rely on horror and violence to sell them, and thus mentally manipulate boys into believing they want things that it is not natural for them to want.

That which is unpleasant, crude or ugly should never be put before small children; they deserve the very best. As a child I recall being absolutely fascinated by a book of fairy stories which had the most intricate and delicate illustrations – I spent much time examining those wonderful pictures, which no doubt helped to establish my appreciation of beauty.

There is a special need for beautifully illustrated books to be available in schools, especially for those children who have little evidence of beauty in their lives, yet when it comes to reading books in Infant schools, I've found that some leave much room for improvement. Either the words or the pictures do not come up to the standards that parents have a right to expect and have trashy subject matter and/or crude illustrations.

Some of the best illustrations I have seen in recent years are those done by Nicola Bayley in *The Mousehole Cat* by Antonia Barber. The book is based on the legend of a Cornish fisherman who braved a fierce storm to catch fish when the villagers of Mousehole were starving. The book is also outstanding in showing a fine example of unselfishness and courage.

A more careful selection of books in Infant Schools could do much to develop a taste for what is good and wholesome, for the younger the child, the more particular we should be in the choice of food that is fed into his thoughts. No attempt should be spared to cherish the purity of a little child's mind. When choosing books for the very young, I read every word and I will not buy a book that has any dubious elements. I look for books with stories that are suited to the child's level of development, which will expand the child's knowledge or imagination, widen his vocabulary and/or reading ability and with good illustrations. Good books are there to be found; all that is needed is an investment of enough time to make a suitable choice.

Right from the earliest age, up to around eight years old, a child's books should be most carefully scrutinised. Further supervision will still be needed after that age, but the reins can then be relaxed.

If we want to nurture compassion in children, they must be sheltered from violence, ugliness and impropriety in their formative years. Children who are properly protected when they are small retain their natural sensitivity to suffering. Seedlings need a protected environment in which to grow sturdily and only when the plant is mature, can it successfully withstand the elements. The same applies to the maturing of a child's thought.

Much soul-searching goes on today about literacy standards so why is there no clamp down on the abbreviated and miss-spelt words and the poor grammar so dear to the hearts of those who write children's comics? Children who are learning to write, and especially those who are struggling to express themselves, are hindered by reading prose that is incorrect.

As children grow older, *what* they are reading is not as significant as the fact that they *are* reading. Enid Blyton, Roald Dalh and J.K. Rowling are to be congratulated on the fact that they have encouraged so many children to get started with reading for pleasure, although we may have some misgivings about Rowling sometimes stretching the limits in her depiction of horror. Series such as The *Horrible Histories* often contain unnecessary horrors and it is regrettable that they are used as school textbooks. If "tweenie" (between childhood and teens) girls are reading the currently popular Jacqueline Wilson's books, then mothers would do well to read them too and be ready to use them to discuss the issues that they raise.

When the teenage years arrive parents should not abdicate their responsibility to keep a watching brief over the diet in magazines as well as books. They would also do well to keep their ears open to the lyrics of pop songs, for teens need help in evaluating what is being presented. Older children will cope with books that will tug at their heartstrings, books like *Greyfriars Bobby* the true story of a dog who lived in Edinburgh and faithfully guarded her master's dead body, but I would never introduce books of that kind before the child was sufficiently mature.

"Children have more need of models than critics" maintained Father Flanagan, who was specially incensed by the corruption of youth by movies, magazines and newspapers. (And that was over a century ago! What would he think now?) "Talk to children behind prison bars", he said, "they will tell you where they got their ideas. Give our children heroes, not villains, to imitate."

Books for Moral Teaching

Traditional stories often provide subject matter that can be used for discussion with young children. Stories like *The Old Woman in the Vinegar Bottle* and *Goldilocks and the Three Bears* provide an opportunity for pointing out the importance of gratitude and respect for privacy, respectively. *The Elves and the Shoemaker* is one of the best ever fairy stories for its example of kind actions and their reward, but be on guard when reading the story of *Little Red Riding Hood.* What happens to the wolf at the end? Is there a picture of him being attacked with an axe? Be cautious also with *The Three Little Pigs.* What happens to the wolf at the end of that one?

Cinderella and other stories that end up with the hero and heroine getting married and then living "happily ever after" open up an opportunity for discussing what makes for a happy marriage.

When I was telling these stories in school, I would ask the children, "What would they have to do to live happily ever after?" "What good qualities would they need?" Politeness, patience, forgiveness etc. – the list could be endless. As children get used to this approach, they will soon be ready with the response that you have to do kind things for the other person and you must talk nicely to them. At the tender age when children start playgroup or school, they are very impressionable and what their teacher tells them may always be remembered. Early instruction of this kind could eventually help to sweeten a marriage or even to save it.

There is one traditional story however, that should be banned forever; that is the tale of *Hansel and Gretel.* The mental pictures it evokes are really repugnant – parents abandoning their children in a wood and a witch who fattens up children before she eats them – such images should have no place in a young child's life. It is a great shame that such a horrid story includes the wonderful idea of a gingerbread house. Maybe someone could write a new story with the delights of a gingerbread house without the inclusion of cannibalism. I find it surprising that Aesop's fables remain in print for so many of them have worthless subject matter.

Hans Christian Anderson is so much more gentle than the brothers Grimm (who live up to their name). I love the line from the story of *Thumbelina* – the little girl who was no bigger than your thumb – "When your heart is full of love you're nine feet tall." *The Ugly Duckling,* the story of a young cygnet's mistaken identity, provides a good opportunity to encourage children to "Judge not according to the appearance, but to judge righteous judgement" as the Bible says. (John 7:24)

Stories should not cut across the child's innate sense of justice. When telling the story of *Jack and the Beanstalk,* I feel on safer ground if I stick to the version that says that the giant had once stolen Jack's mother's money when Jack was a baby, so when Jack finds the hen that lays the golden eggs, he was only getting back what the giant had, in effect, previously taken from them. Whenever I read this story to my own children and got to the bit that says, "Jack was a lazy boy and wouldn't do much work for his mother at home, but he was kind hearted" one of the children would always interrupt and say, "He couldn't have been kind hearted, else he would have helped his mother" and I would have to agree that the writer got it wrong.

The story of the *Little Red Hen* who got no help from her friends in the various stages of bread making and so would not share the finished loaf with them, points out the advantages of helping others. The story of *Pinnochio,* whose nose grew long when he told lies, can be a useful cautionary tale.

One of the best books for providing children with positive role models for politeness, is, sadly, out of print as I write. This is Richard Scarry's *Please and Thank You Book* which is delightful for its light but positive moral touch. Heroes like Huckle Cat and Lowly Worm were thoughtful of their Little Sister. We get such gems as

Then all the children went off to school. Little Sister's shoelace came untied. Everybody waited while Lowly tied it for her.

At the supper table, everybody ate with his fork. Nobody ever eats with his fingers or his foot.

In the story of *Pig Will and Pig Won't*, in the same book, we read, "Mother Pig had two little pigs – Pig Will and Pig Won't. Whenever she asked them to do something, Pig Will said 'I will.' But Pig Won't always said, 'I won't!'" One day Daddy Pig asked the two little pigs to come to the boatyard to help him work on his boat. The upshot of the tale is that Pig Will had a great day helping his Daddy and Pig Won't "began to understand that work – especially of you are helping others – can be lots more fun than doing nothing." We could do with loads more books like this and it is good to see a TV adaptation.

I am always sorry when stories tell of something going wrong for a child and "she cried and cried and cried". I was delighted once to come across a story about a little boy named Alan who was very fond of hats. One day when he was out with his mother he lost a special hat that his granddad had given him. We didn't get tears, but instead, "Alan didn't cry. 'You are a good boy, Alan' said his mother." Its a joy to find a story that gives examples of children who did not give way to disappointment, then right from an early age children can be encouraged to face their problems instead of giving way to them.

Where the Wild Things Are by Maurice Sendak encourages facing your problems. The hero, Max, has been sent to his bedroom and imagines himself sailing away to visit a world of friendly monsters – but when things get out of hand, Max told the wild things, "Be still" and tamed them by staring into their eyes.

I don't like stories that glorify naughtiness, even if the ending adjusts the balance and I have never told stories from *My Naughty Little Sister* books for this reason. The tone of some stories makes naughtiness sound important and attractive and I find some of the *Mr. Men* books by Roger Hargreaves disappointing in this respect.

Its interesting to see how the *Milly-Molly-Mandy* books which emphasise goodness without moralising, are still around and how Enid Blyton, defying what the so-called experts say about her, remains on the shelves, for children still enjoy her stories with their sound moral values. One story called *The Singing Kettle* is about a kettle that sang every time its owner, a mean pixie, told lies to avoid helping people. When the pixie started to be kind, to stop the kettle telling tales about him, we read, "he suddenly felt very nice inside. It was lovely to give somebody something. It made him feel warm and kind." Here's a fine starting point for a discussion. Do the children know that feeling? If not, suggest they do kind things and discover how nice it feels.

It is far too difficult to locate books that give specific instances of characters going out of their way to be kind to others in children's books, but I found just one in the story of *Dogger,* by Shirley Hughes. Dogger was a toy dog who was much loved by Dave, the little boy who owned him. One day, Dogger was lost and turned up for sale on a second-hand stall at a fair, but was sold whilst Dave and his big sister Bella had gone to get some money to buy him back. Bella finally got Dogger back by asking the little girl who had bought him, to swap him for a big teddy bear. We read that Dave "hugged Dogger and he hugged Bella round the waist. 'Thank you, Bella' he said."

The Dr. Seuss books are wonderful nonsense stories which develop a child's sense of humour and are unfailingly popular. Possibly the best for giving a good example in caring for others, is *Horton Hears a Who!* Horton is an elephant who bravely defends the very small inhabitants of a speck of dust on a clover flower. The story teaches that small people have to make themselves heard and that big people should listen. The series on *Frog and Toad* by Arnold Lobel also shows kindness between creatures, for frog and toad are true friends who help each other.

One of the best books to be published for young children in the 1990s must be the award winning *Rainbow Fish,* followed by its sequel, *The Rainbow Fish to the Rescue.* In the first book, the little rainbow fish had scales of every colour under the rainbow, but was conceited about her beauty so was shunned by the other fish. When she shared her scales with them all and the whole shoal had one little coloured scale, she was really happy. She discovered the real value of personal beauty and friendship. In the second book the rainbow fish saves a little striped fish from becoming a shark's dinner. These books are expensive, but they are beautifully produced and are worth their weight in gold.

Discretion dictates that we be very careful when selecting Bible stories to be told to children. One little boy, who had just had a baby sister came home from school very distressed, for the teacher had told the story of the baby Moses who was put in the bulrushes to save him from the king who was drowning new-born babies. Apart from Bible stories, there are few children's stories that mention God in a meaningful way. One that does is *Travis Talks with God* by Jack Thornton. This tells the story of how a little boy who was sledging fell off in the snow and hurt himself and then wondered why God hadn't looked after him. He then remembered that an inner voice had told him to slow down, but he had failed to obey. He then realised that God had been looking after him all the time and made the resolve that in future he would listen to God more carefully and do what He said.

C.S. Lewis' *Narnia* books are in a class of their own in their ability to capture a child's imagination and at the same time to open a spiritual dimension. They offer scope for fruitful discussion.

It is important, especially in the early years, to make quite clear to children whether a story is true or not and if it is a true story, to know when and where it happened. In Communist Russia, the film *Oliver* was popular with young people, who were led to believe that it depicted the life of children in Britain today and the young Russians felt really sorry for the British children who had such shabby clothes and so little food!

Feeding right thoughts into young minds is giving children the correct tools to think with, just as we would give children the correct tools for any other job they are learning to do.

The consummation of all culture is the love of the beautiful.

Plato

Nursery (and other) Rhymes

In the home and in playgroups and nursery schools, nursery rhymes are often the first introduction to our literary heritage, yet some of them have very dubious backgrounds. Lucy Locket and Kitty Fisher were apparently prostitutes and *Ring-a-ring o'roses* describes the symptoms and effects of the plague, but children don't know about these things and neither do most of the adults who sing or read the rhymes to them. I don't find much to quarrel with there but I do with this:

There was a little man
And he had a little gun
And his bullets were made of lead, lead, lead.

He saw a little duck
And he got his little gun
And he shot it through the middle of the head, head, head.

The tune is light and catchy but the subject matter is entirely inappropriate for small children. Then there is *Ding Dong Bell,* with its tale of pussy in the well and the naughty boy who tried to drown the poor pussy cat. Equally bad is:

Bye Baby Bunting
Daddy's gone a hunting.
He's gone to get a rabbit skin
To wrap his Baby Bunting in.

I find it disturbing that we continue to print such offensive rhymes and present them to little children. *Sing a Song of Sixpence* is a marginal case:

Sing a song of sixpence
A pocketful of rye.
Four and twenty blackbirds baked in a pie.
When the pie was opened, the birds began to sing,
Wasn't that a dainty dish to set before the king?

The king was in his counting house,
Counting out his money.
The queen was in the parlour,
Eating bread and honey.
The maid was in the garden,
Hanging out the clothes,
When down came a blackbird and pecked off her nose!

Children can be told that this is all stuff and nonsense; also that no blackbird could really peck off your nose.

Some nursery rhymes, such as *Three blind mice,* can easily be amended:

Three blind mice, three blind mice,
See how they run! See how they run!
They all ran after the farmer's wife,
Who cut off their tails with the carving knife.
Did every you see such a thing in your life
As three blind mice.

People are so used to this familiar rhyme, that they don't seem to give the words one moment's thought, for if they did think about them, they would surely rebel! In our family we taught what we thought was an original adaptation of *Three blind mice* only to find later that someone had preceded us by 100 years. Our version went like this:

Three kind mice, three kind mice.
See how they run! See how they run!
They all ran after the farmer's wife,
Who cut them some cheese with the carving knife.

Did ever you see such a thing in your life,
As three kind mice.

We also had a go at improving another:

Upstairs, downstairs
In my lady's chamber.
There I met an old man
Who wouldn't say his prayers,
So I took him by the left leg
And threw him down the stairs,

We changed the last two lines to read:

I took him by the left arm
And helped him down the stairs.

The trouble with this is that the illustration in the book won't tie in with your improved words. Parents and teachers can always do their own adaptations, but publishers of nursery rhymes should take a closer look at some of the things they are putting into print. After all, if people have been adapting them for one hundred years, it could be time they took the hint.

Little children love poetry and especially nonsense poetry – which is what nursery rhymes are. A.A. Milne's poems have that touch of fantasy so essential to sparking off the imagination. No child should grow up in ignorance of the three little foxes who kept their handkerchiefs in cardboard boxes, nor of the King who wanted butter for his breakfast. What great fun too can be had reading such nonsense as Edward Lear wrote in *The Owl and the Pussy Cat*, *The Jumblies* (who went to sea in a sieve) and *The Quangle Wangle's Hat*. I have two favourite short nonsense poems, which children love. I do not know who wrote either of them, but they are:

I eat my peas with honey,
I've done it all my life.
It makes the peas taste funny,
But it keeps them on my knife.

I've never seen a purple cow.
I never hope to see one.
But this I'll tell you anyhow,
I'd rather see than be one.

The Moving Image

The Judeo-Christian based morality in our society has been abandoned in favour of the politically correct non-judgmental creed that 'anything goes' and all this is having disastrous consequences for all of us.   Leo McKinstry, (referring to TV)

Moving images, which are imprinted on the mind more vividly than pictures in books, provide an area of concern that grows more challenging as the years go by. At first we only had films, then came TV and video followed by computer games, some with violent themes and sexual innuendo, and now pornography, not only on the Internet, but seeping more into mainstream films. Video and film classification is an area of special concern, especially as the target market for pornography is getting younger. Studies done in France have uncovered the fact that a substantial proportion of ten year olds have watched pornographic videos and there is concern that a diet of porn has been a factor in the increase in gang rape amongst school children.

Videos which at one time would have been banned, now have a special classification to be sold in licensed outlets only. But once these are purchased, they can be seen by whomsoever the owner pleases and the fact is that it pleases some to show them to children. This does raise the question of whether a civilised society should permit such material to be produced at all.

Parents in the 1960s and 1970s had less to cope with than parents today, but an area that worried many were film trailers which in those days did not have the same rating as the main picture. I became increasingly concerned about what our young family might see in trailers when we went to the cinema. On one occasion I complained directly to the British Board of Film Censors, whose secretary then was John Trevelyan. We exchanged some correspondence and an excerpt from one letter that Mr. Trevelyan sent to me is still worth noting. He wrote, "The film industry is narrow minded, but this relates almost entirely to the desire to make commercial profits. If sex films sell better than other films they will make them; when the public gets sick of them, if they ever do, they will stop making them."

This letter was interesting in its use of the phrase "narrow minded" – used, I would say, in a more correct sense than is usually the case. The letter also showed the crux of the whole matter – that the standard of the entertainment industry is actually in the hands of the public. Finally I went to see Mr. Trevelyan who told me that many of the things I was saying had also been said by Mary Whitehouse who had visited him earlier. I always had a tremendous admiration for Mary Whitehouse for her courage in standing firm for what she knew to be right, despite all the insults and abuse that were hurled at her. How many, like myself, were grateful that she was there and also wondered that if she hadn't been there, would our concerns have led any of us into taking her role? Would we have had the courage and tenacity that she showed?

In Mary Whitehouse's book, *A Most Dangerous Woman?* there is a touching scene of a meeting, arranged by Mrs. Whitehouse, between Harman Grisewood, then Deputy Director General of the BBC, and a girl called Pauline. Pauline and her younger sister were living with their grandmother following the break-up of their parents' marriage. She asked Mr Grisewood, "Don't you think it would be wonderful if the BBC could put on plays which would help families like ours to stay together, instead of ones in which, whenever there's trouble, people fly for a cigarette or a drink or out through the front door?" TV is a medium that has such potential for good and for helping people to solve their problems, that it is one of the saddest things when it is tarnished by trash. Maybe we need more Paulines to press the case.

TV soaps are an obvious vehicle that can be used for helping people to solve their problems. The BBC has used radio soap opera for this purpose, not in the UK but in Afghanistan where the programme *New Home, New Life* had a large following. The Head of the BBC Afghan Education Project was quoted as saying, "We are trying to educate in the context of Afghan culture and Islamic religion." In 2002 the British government invested in a TV soap for Africa called *Heart and Soul* which was aimed at halting the spread of AIDS. If the BBC and the government see the value of such projects for overseas, couldn't more be done in the UK to inspire social morality? Couldn't more be done to halt the tide of teenage promiscuity and drug taking and to reinstate our Christian values? The potential for good is just enormous.

One hopeful step in the right direction has been the way in which *Coronation Street* has tackled the problem of teenage pregnancy with its depiction of Sarah, who became a teenage mother. The story line left viewers in no doubt that casual sex is wrong and that it leads to many horrendous difficulties; it also illustrated the strength of a loving, caring family.

We hear much, and rightly so, about the harm caused by the proliferation of sex and violence on TV, but little about the rudeness and lack of respect of young adults for their parents in some TV dramas where youngsters are frequently insolent, thoughtless and arrogant. When small children watch such behaviour it counteracts the standards that many parents are trying to instil. A comment that seems typical of the attitude of TV producers was voiced by a spokesman who said, "As producers of contemporary drama, I believe it would be absolutely remiss of us to portray young people in anything less than a 'real' and therefore identifiable context." What is conveniently overlooked is that by no means all young people treat their parents with disrespect, so why can't they show a few more polite ones? The reason would no doubt be that they believe it wouldn't make such compelling viewing.

Allowing children to have televisions, and computers too, in their bedrooms is fraught with danger. The trouble is that technology has raced ahead of many parents, but not of their computer-savvy offspring. Parents need to wake up to the temptations inherent in this practice. At what cost are they meekly assenting to the pressure to go along with what other parents are doing? Sexual situations stimulate curiosity and help to destroy innate modesty; violence in real life situations encourages real life violence and violence in futuristic films engenders a feeling of powerlessness. It is hard to know which of these is the most harmful.

Some parents say that their children should know what goes on in the world. Joyce Grenfell had the best answer to that one. She said, "People say 'These things really happen'. Well, so does diarrhoea, but that doesn't mean I want to see it on the stage." Because some perverted and sick things are happening, there is no need to watch them and especially no need for the young to see them. Young people should not be educated into perversion, sadism or brutality. Such obnoxious food should not be the diet of any right thinking person, and certainly not of juveniles.

Frances Lawrence, widow of Philip Lawrence, the London headmaster who was murdered in December 1995 by a teenager armed with a knife, wrote about the media, "[They] have a responsibility to face up to the consequences of their increasing reliance on an insidious barbarity in so many outlets." She then mentioned "the casual violence of too many children's programmes, cartoons and computer games." The majority of computer games may not be violent, but the extent of the violence in those that are, is appalling, for example, one called *Grand Theft Auto* gives points for running people over and killing those who try to stop you stealing.

Is it surprising that a Home Office Report published in 1997 linked video violence with aggressive behaviour among violent offenders? Many of us marvel that the link between video "entertainment" fed into youngsters' minds, and violence in our communities should warrant an official report at all, for the link was obvious after it was revealed that the young murderers of James Bulger had been fed on a diet of horror videos and replicated scenes from one of them. The film *Clockwork Orange* was withdrawn from cinema screens by its director, Stanley Kubrick, after copy-cat incidents were reported.

Like many other facets of society today, there are no easy answers to the challenges presented by the media especially whilst the love of money, no matter what the human cost, remains the motivating factor for many producers. The answer must surely lie in patiently educating the young to have better expectations from the entertainment they are getting. Parents should be ready to open up discussions about the films the family sees and hopefully help youngsters to become discerning and discriminating. Many films today are technically and photographically brilliant but what about the content? What good qualities did the characters show? Was there a deeper lesson to be learned from the story line? What kind of motivation did the characters show? Were they people you would admire? It is always good to pick out the films with characters who are positive examples. These range from the fictional *Casablanca* to the real life *Erin Brokovitch*. Erin Brokovitch is a single mum who stood up to a giant corporation in America and won, and in *Casablanca*, the hero Rick Blaine has the vision to perceive the enduring satisfaction brought about by acting ethically.

A great blessing to today's young mothers are the many excellent educational videos for young children. The advent of *Teletubbies* marked a turning point on the tele-horizon, for the Teletubbies send positive messages to little children, like not being discouraged if you fail the first time, not being frightened, and, above all, being nice to each other. (Have you noticed how few fictional characters on TV are nice to each other?) All over Britain, little children at playgroups started giving each other "big hugs" like the Teletubbies do.

Let's Do Something!

Should we now stand up and say, Enough? We, the public, will no longer buy, read, or watch this corrosive stuff.   Anna Ford

For better or for worse, we all contribute to the mental environment in which corrosive entertainment is being marketed and this environment at times can seem like a heavy black cloud. Each of us can work to dispel that cloud and we should feel empowered by the knowledge that there are many thinking people who share our concerns, but who, alas, too often remain silent. **DON'T KEEP SILENT!** This book was written because I couldn't keep silent.

Do we really want corrosive stuff on cinema screens, TV, video and the Internet? If the answer is "No", then it is up to us to do something about it. A film critic said recently that the British Board of Film Classification gets away with its permissive policy by stealth only because most of us don't kick up a fuss. If you are a parent, or even if you're not, SPEAK OUT about the things in society that are harmful to the rising generation. Sometimes a group of parents taking a stand together about what their children should or should not see on TV and videos, can help relieve the peer pressure that otherwise threatens to become intolerable. Be ready to take the lead and you will be sure to find other parents who will be grateful to you.

If you have reached retirement years you have more flexibility in the way in which you can use your time, and are in a good position to look out for ways in which you can help to uplift the tone of your community. Don't be intimidated by the subtle, or not so subtle, wording used to promote so-called adult entertainment. "Not for the easily offended" or similar wording is used in an attempt to make those who are not attracted by vulgarity, feel naive and unsophisticated.

When Bruce Gyngell, managing director of Tyne Tees Television took the decision to drop the series *Hollywood Lovers* from his region, so many people wrote to him applauding his decision that he said he was quite overwhelmed with the positive support. Letters and a telephone poll conducted by the *Yorkshire Post* revealed that 87% supported the stand he had taken, with a mere 13% against. A 2001 telephone poll during a *Heaven and Earth Show* to answer the question, "Is the media corrupting society?" elicited over 7,000 calls, the second highest response ever and 92% said it was. A teletext poll which asked the question, "Are you sick of TV sleaze?" got a 97% yes vote. Other polls have shown support for stronger safeguards to protect children from seeing violence and sex on the media.

Complains about sex and violence in TV soaps have been increasing and in 2001 the Broadcasting Standards Commission ordered a clean up. Maybe this influenced the more responsible approach to teen pregnancy in Coronation Street already mentioned.

Even small numbers of people with commitment and devotion can galvanise the many. Margaret Mead once said, "Never doubt that a small group of thoughtful, committed citizens can change the world. Indeed, it's the only thing that ever has." All social reforms have started with the vision of one individual who would not let up because of an inner conviction of the rightness of a cause, and as a social activist of many years standing I have been quite amazed to discover what a difference just one person can make.

Sometimes it takes only one person to protest about obnoxious books or magazines in order to get something done. A comparatively small number can get offensive posters removed. Complaining about inappropriate scenes on TV is tougher, as most TV bosses seem to be hell bent on pushing the boundaries of the public acceptance of indecency and violence and numbers do help here. You can get support and information by joining mediawatch-uk whose address is given at the end of this chapter.

More people are needed to take a stand for decency, and to keep a watchful eye on posters, shop windows, advertisements, magazines, television etc. When you see images that are pleasing and constructive, do you write and express your appreciation? It is so rewarding to companies and individuals to know that someone appreciates what they do. On the other hand, if you see things that violate good taste and decency, do you write to the organisation concerned stating clearly why it is that you are objecting and saying what you would like to be done about it? For each person who takes the trouble to protest, there are probably as many as fifty who feel just the same, but didn't take the time or the trouble to speak up. Customers are vital to any business, and no one should want to offend their customers, but if your protest is ignored, do persist.

A Salvation Army lady I knew had a novel answer to dealing with offensive material. One day when she went into her local paper shop, she was dismayed to find a selection of salacious picture postcards prominently displayed. When she complained to the shop's new owner he said he didn't like them either but had found them stashed away and wanted to turn them into cash. "Is this all you've got?" she asked. It was, and when he said that he didn't intend to buy more, she bought the lot and put them all into her dustbin. "I regarded it as a donation to my church," she said. The man got his money and she got the cards out of circulation; both were satisfied.

It's not so easy, however, to stop something that has a wider circulation, but it can be done if you are determined and persistent. A leading children's comic once offered free packs of "rappers." These were little cardboard disks with pictures on, that were highly prized by children at that time. They played games with them and swapped them with friends. One mother was appalled to discover that out of the five free rappers her son got, two had truly repulsive pictures, one was of a monster with a stake through his head and blood gushing out.

A phone call to the publishers of the comic uncovered the fact that they had not realised the nature of the contents but felt powerless to do anything about it because they had already advertised that rappers would be given away for the next four weeks. Undeterred, the mother persisted until she found out where the offending disks came from (they were from Israel) and finally got further importation stopped. A good place to start raising matters of concern is in the letters columns of papers and magazines and it's worth remembering that it's always easier to get a letter into a local rather than a national paper.

If you are a shopkeeper, are you comfortable with the items you are selling? One newsagent I know was not happy to sell near-pornographic magazines, so cancelled the order when he took over the shop. He has remained unmoved by the grumbles of those who would have bought the offending publications and rewarded by the gratitude of the mothers who bring their children into the shop.

Some situations call for changes in the law, e.g. over obscenity. Our obscenity laws are out of date and we need more people to lobby their MPs about the issue. Surprisingly few people go to see their MP's about matters of ethical concern. If you do so, it can help to take one or two others with you, so you have witnesses. Take the right attitude too. Don't be confrontational, but be prepared to discuss and to question, "Do you think . . . is right, for we're not happy about it?" Do your homework and be in possession of the facts. MPs are busy people and it helps if you take a letter with you confirming the points you raised and asking for a written reply.

If what you are doing is right, never be tempted to think it is a lost cause; it may take time, but eventually you can expect to win through. Every battle can be won with right on your side, for eventually more will join you and the voice of the people must finally be heard. We can also pray for film directors, for TV bosses and for writers and journalists, pray that their eyes be opened to motivate them to act with greater integrity, sensitivity and refinement.

Be not overcome of evil, but overcome evil with good.

Romans 12:21

USEFUL ADDRESSES

For comments or complaints about the content of films or trailers or their classification:

British Board of Film and Video Classification
3 Soho Square
LONDON W1V 6HD
Tel. 020 7440 1570
Fax. 020 7287 0141
Website: www.bbfc.co.uk

To contact your MP:

House of Commons
LONDON SW1A OAA
Tel. 020 7219 3000

Always ask your MP to kindly forward your letter to the Department of Culture, Media & Sport, also to the Home Office.

To comment or complain about the content of a television or radio programme or to obtain a copy of the Commission's Code of Guidance:

Broadcasting Standards Commission
7 The Sanctuary
LONDON SW1P 3JS
Tel. 020 7808 1000
Fax. 020 7233 0397
Website: www.bsc.org.uk

The BSC publishes annual statistics on the comments received.

To make a comment about a BBC programme:

BBC Telephone Service
Tel. 08700 100 222 (national rate)

To comment about independent radio programmes:

Radio Authority
Holbrook House
14 Great Queen Street
LONDON WC2B 5DG

To comment about an independent TV programme or TV advertisements:

Independent TV Commission (ITC)
3 Foley Street,
London W1P 7LB
Tel. 020 7255 3000
Fax. 020 7306 7800
E-mail: viewer.relations@itc.org.uk

To contact the government department responsible for broadcasting:

Department of Culture, Media and Sport
2-4 Cockspur Street
LONDON SW1Y SDH
Tel. 0207211 6000
E-mail enquiries@culture.gov.uk
Website: www.culture.gov.uk

To get a list of TV & radio addresses and phone numbers:

Mediawatch–uk
3 Willow House
Kennington Road,
ASHFORD, Kent, TN24 ONR
Tel. 01233 633936
Fax. 01233 633836
E-mail: Info@mediawatchuk.org
Website: www.mediawatchuk.org

To support parents who are campaigning to persuade the media that they
have a responsibility to uphold moral values:

Mediamarch
PO Box 353
Cheltenham Glos. GL53 7ZQ
Tel. 020 8467 6452
Website: www.mediamarch.org.uk

For complaints about the Internet:

Internet Watch Foundation
East View
5 Coles Lane,
Oakington,
CAMBRIDGE CB4 5BA
Tel. 01223 237700
Fax. 01223 235870
E-mail admin@iwf.org.uk
Website: www.internetwatcg.org.uk

For comments or complaints about public advertising (except for TV):

The Advertising Standards Authority Ltd
2 Torrington Place
LONDON WC1E 7HW
Tel. 020 7580 5555
Fax. 020 7631 3051
Website: www.asa.org.uk

It should be noted that it is not the practice of the Advertising Standards Authority to deal with shop window displays or point of sale material. If you find an offensive display in a shop, or in its window, take it up with the shop concerned, and if you don't get satisfaction, approach your local Trading Standards department whose address and telephone number may be obtained from your Town Hall.

Afterword: Our Children's Heritage

The Bible is the learned man's masterpiece, the ignorant man's
dictionary, the wise man's directory.   Mary Baker Eddy

Some years ago a Jamaican clergyman, newly arrived in Britain, was visiting
our home. "Is England as you expected it to be?" I asked him. To my horror,
he said that England was not at all what he expected and he was bitterly
disappointed. "Why?" I asked. "You send missionaries to my country, so I
thought England was a Christian country" he replied, "Now I get here and I
find it's not. You need your missionaries here."

Others who are disturbed by what is happening in our society today and
who are concerned about the behaviour and attitudes of the young, cry out
and say we need a new philosophy. We don't. All we need to do is to
understand better the one on which western society has been built, to
appreciate what it has done for the advancement of civilisation and to make
it more practical to our children.

We have become apathetic about our rich cultural heritage which is
rooted in Christianity. We take it for granted that justice should be fair and
tempered with mercy, that we should have concern for the welfare of others
and that there should be respect for minority views. What many people fail
to realise is that we have these expectations because we grew up in an
environment where Christianity has long been the dominant religion,
however imperfectly practised. It would seem that people have forgotten
that long before the state was involved, Christians founded the first schools
and hospitals and provided the first social workers who aided the poor and
the deprived. We have grown up in a country where the Christian precepts
for living have been taught for generations in our Sunday Schools and in
our day schools and children are noticeably the poorer now this is no longer
the case.

During the latter part of the twentieth century Christian holy days were
progressively phased out. Whitsuntide is now the Spring Bank holiday and
Ascension Day is almost forgotten. Christmas has been hijacked for
commercial ends and its significance becomes hard for children to
comprehend when Santa becomes its focal point instead of the coming of
Jesus Christ. Easter is now associated with eggs and a bunny, and the
crucifixion and resurrection are increasingly being marginalised.

Muslims study the Koran and know long passages by heart. Why don't more Christians have the same dedication to the Bible? The Bible combines incomparable wisdom with practical common sense, it offers guidance on social relations and bringing up children; it has guided and comforted countless thousands and, most important of all, it reveals an ever-present but unseen power for good and teaches how to utilise that power.

The Bible is the world's best-seller and people have risked their lives to have it and, even in the twentieth century, have *given* their lives so that others may read it. Western art, architecture, music and literature have all been profoundly influenced by the Bible and cannot be properly appreciated without a knowledge of its contents. Wonderful and exciting stories, which teach valuable lessons, are found within its pages. The story of David, the shepherd boy who slayed the giant Goliath, gives encouragement not to be afraid even when a problem seems too big to handle and that with right on your side, you can win. It is a great story and children love it. Yet when the Ministry of Health wanted to use the David and Goliath theme for posters to combat AIDS, research showed that the story wasn't sufficiently well known and a different theme had to be chosen. At one time every child and every adult in the country would have known that story.

Sometimes it takes first-hand experience of non-Christian cultures to bring home the value of our own traditions. A man who was out east in the 1950s told me of a time when he was near a fast flowing river. There was a bridge over this river where a crowd of Chinese people were laughing and enjoying themselves, so he went to see what was entertaining them. He was not prepared for what he saw; a man was being swept downstream, waving his arms and crying for help, but none was forthcoming, for the Oriental mind had not been enlightened by compassion.

Doctor Ernest Gordon, who was a Japanese prisoner of war in World War II, wrote in his book, *Miracle on the River Kwai*:

Usually as we marched through villages we were treated with indifference and contempt. A man dying by the road was left to die. There was no place for mercy in their philosophy.

But once we came to a village where we received a treatment so different that it astonished us. There was mercy in the eyes of those who rushed to the roadside to watch us go by. Before we had reached the end of their settlement they were back, laden with cakes, bananas, eggs, medicines and money which they thrust into our hands. Later we learnt that this village had been converted to Christianity by missionaries.

In the 21st century increasing numbers have given up on the Christian ideal, there are fewer and fewer Sunday Schools and possibly of even graver consequences, many state schools have progressively weakened religious education by separating it from the Bible. The presence, in some areas, of a large number of children from non-Christian backgrounds has been deemed sufficient reason to water down religious instruction to the level of personal and social values which are bereft of a Supreme Being. Contemporary Religious Studies have a broadly based approach which has removed the framework in which to make personal moral decisions, and turned religion into a doctrinal theory with subject matter so diversified that it lacks both focus and substance.

Under the 1944 Education Act, religious education was the only subject that was compulsory in schools, a situation that came under strong attack from humanists in the teaching profession who were especially vocal during the late 1960s. A Secular Education leaflet published in that period demanded that children be taught "only what is capable of universal verification according to the highest standards available to each generation." This sounded very plausible and few people seemed to realise that a daily act of worship in school was initiated by our Victorian forefathers who knew the value of starting each day with prayer. Teachers seldom pointed out to children that this is why prayers start the school day – though in my experience, children were interested to learn it – and it's safe to say that as the majority of teachers were not in the habit of praying they weren't in a position to judge its value and were all too easily swayed by the materialistically based logic of the humanists.

The quality of religious education has further declined because social conditions were no longer conducive to producing sufficient teachers competent to teach it. The "daily act of worship" which was also compulsory under the 1944 Act frequently deteriorated into less frequent assemblies dominated in the main by school business. According to the Office for Standards in Education, 70% of secondary schools flout the law in this respect.

Why are we phasing out the Christian holy book when, according to the 1988 Education Reform Act, religious education and school assemblies "shall be wholly or mainly of a broadly Christian character"? "Religious Education addresses the search for meaning and fulfilment in life" states the introduction in one local Education Authority R.I. Syllabus, which then outlines a programme which barely touches on the one book, which, more than any other, reveals the way to a fulfilling and meaningful life!

When we teach history, we don't teach about how they learnt history in times gone by, we teach about rulers, battles and social conditions of the past. When we teach geography, we don't teach about how geography is taught in other countries, we teach about mountains, rivers, continents and cities. How is it that religious education teaches what other people teach about their religions, instead of dealing with what religion is all about, namely, GOD? I once asked a group of six formers who were studying RI for A-levels if their course included studying the nature of God. "Oh no" they replied, "we don't do that sort of thing at all!" I cannot imagine such slip-shod methods being accepted in any other subject.

I sincerely hope that the examples used in this book have served to illustrate that an understanding of the nature of God is of practical value in the raising of good children. I hope that I have opened up the value of the Bible as a child-rearing manual and shown how it is adaptable to today's rapidly changing world. I trust that parents will find that the idea of God as a divine Mind is a concept that helps them in rearing their children and that it will help to alleviate fears for their children's wellbeing. As children learn to practice the Bible's timeless precepts and rely on the guidance of their heavenly Father-Mother, their future will be bright with promise.

> I am going to use wise sayings . . . from the past, things we have heard and known. . . . We will not keep them from our children; We will tell the next generation about the Lord's power and his great deeds and the wonderful things he has done.
>
> Psalm 78:2-4, GNB

Bibliography

Bennett, William J (1993), *The Book of Virtues, A Treasury of Great Moral Stories,* (Edited with Commentary by Bennett, William J), Simon & Schuster, New York, NY.

Burgess, Alan (1970), *The Small Woman,* Pan Books.

Cruz, Nicky (2003), *Run Baby Run,* Hodder & Stoughton Religious.

Dalai Lama (1991), *Freedom in Exile,* Sphere Books, 1990.

Drummond, Henry (1947), *The Greatest Thing in the World,* Hodder & Stoughton.

Eddy, Mary Baker (1994), *Science and Health with Key to the Scriptures,* The Writings of Mary Baker Eddy   (See also www.spirituality.com.)

Morgan, Mary Kimball (1965), *Education at the Principia,* Principia.

Oursler, Fulton and Oursler, Will (1950), *Father Flanagan of Boy's Town,* Kingswood, Surrey.

Pullinger, Jackie with Quicke, Andrew (1980), *Chasing the Dragon,* Hodder & Stoughton Educational, London.

Whitehouse, Mary (1982), *A Most Dangerous Woman?,* Lion Publishing.

Wilkerson, David (1963), *The Cross and the Switchblade,* Pyramid Books.

Wyndham, John (1994), *The Ultimate Freedom,* Mountain Top Productions.

Some of these books may not available through mainstream bookshops but may be obtained from:

The Art Store
18 Main Street
Kirkby Lonsdale
Cumbria
LA6 2AG,

or in the USA from

The Mail Box
9101 Lakehurst Drive
Oaklahoma City
Oaklahoma
73120
USA